# ESTATE PLANNING
## AND
# ADMINISTRATION

# ESTATE PLANNING

### AND

# ADMINISTRATION

*How to Maximize Assets, Minimize Taxes, and Protect Loved Ones*

**Edmund T. Fleming, C.P.A., J.D.**

ALLWORTH PRESS
NEW YORK

**Praise for *Estate Planning and Administration***

"Law attorney and certified public accountant Fleming adds a new title to the arsenal of resources on estate planning. Presenting the process as a series of decisions to be made, he methodically provides the information needed to make them. Fleming covers wills, trusts, income and estate taxes, powers of attorney, and the responsibilities of executors and administrators. Each chapter begins with a "points to consider" section containing practical tips, observations, and numerous checklists to help readers assemble documents and understand processes. The appendixes include sample wills, powers of attorney, living trusts, a glossary, and a directory of information sources . . . this book is good preparation for a meeting with estate-planning professionals."

—*The Library Journal*

"Coping with the loss of a loved one is beset with stress and confusion. Grief is a heavy burden, yet most families are further saddled with the responsibility of administering the estate. For those who find themselves in this situation and for those who wish to shield loved ones from it, *Estate Planning and Administration* is a comprehensive guide for making this subject as simple as possible. The book covers the steps to developing an estate plan, tax issues, federal requirements, and sample forms to fill out, and includes checklists and examples. The author is a CPA attorney specializing in real estate and estate planning."

—*Working Money*

*I would like to dedicate this book to my wife, Fran,*
*who spent countless hours proofreading the manuscript*
*and provided valuable insight and many suggestions for the book.*
*Also, to my three wonderful daughters, Therese, Katie, and Patricia,*
*who think it is kind of cool that their dad wrote a book.*

05   04   03   02   01          5   4   3   2

Published by Allworth Press
An imprint of Allworth Communications
10 East 23rd Street, New York, NY 10010

Cover design by Douglas Design Associates, New York, NY

Page composition/typography by SR Desktop Services, Ridge, NY

Library of Congress Cataloging-in-Publication Data
Fleming, Edmund T.
    Estate planning and administration : how to maximize assets,
  minimize taxes, and protect loved ones / Edmund T. Fleming
        p.    cm.
    Includes index.
    ISBN 1-58115-083-0
    1. Estate planning—United States.   I. Title.
  KF750.F59   2001
  346.7305'2—dc21                              2001022317

Printed in Canada

# TABLE OF CONTENTS

# Update: The Economic Growth and Tax Relief Reconciliation Act of 2001

On the first page of *Estate Planning & Administration*, I wrote that "with inflation, changes in family structure, and new laws passed each year, you should review your estate plan at least once a year." True to form, Congress and the President enacted new legislation to make our lives just a little more complicated. On June 7, 2001, President Bush signed into law a $1.35 trillion tax cut bill, Public Law 107-16, "The Economic Growth and Tax Relief Reconciliation Act of 2001." Most of the tax changes are scheduled to be phased in over several years, with full repeal of the current estate tax scheduled for January 1, 2010.

While this sounds logical enough, the law actually has some bizarre provisions. For example, due to budget constraints, the estate tax will be fully repealed on January 1, 2010, but that repeal will last for only one year. Unless further legislation is passed, on December 31, 2010, the current estate tax rates will go back into effect. What a conundrum! Is it repealed or not?

Due to several factors explained below, this new law increases the need for proper estate planning as explained in this book. This law will require increased record keeping and planning. For example, on page 11, I suggested saving income tax returns for three years. I now suggest that all tax returns should be saved. Prior year's tax returns may help accountants and executors in future years calculate what is known as your basis for property.

As expected, this new law was passed with great public fanfare and with many politicians claiming that they were siding with the American taxpayers by saving them lots of money. Many people are claiming that since the "death" tax will be eliminated in 2010, everyone can look forward to spending their inheritances without worrying about giving Uncle Sam a share. Please be careful. As passed, this new law requires that a person actually die in the year 2010 in order not to have to pay any estate taxes. This new law also left intact the Gift Tax laws and did not decrease income taxes on accumulated balances in deferred compensation plans or Individual Retirement Accounts, which are becoming the most significant assets for many people.

Today, if you inherit property and immediately sell it, there are no income taxes due on the sale since your basis in the property is "stepped-up" to its fair market value in the estate (as defined on page 160). Starting in 2010, there will be no stepped-up basis for property. If one of your estate planning objectives is the equitable distribution of property between your children as discussed on page 17, you definitely will want to annually update your key document files (page 9) to ensure that one beneficiary does not end up paying substantially more in income taxes on inherited property than another beneficiary.

Remember that there are reasons to consider the trusts explained in this book in your estate plan for purposes other than saving Federal estate taxes. Even after the estate tax is repealed in 2010, you should consider trusts to protect property, ease estate administration, help avoid probate, and provide the necessary income for life for a spouse or a dependent. Some people who have already included various irrevocable (cannot be changed) trusts in their estate plans may now attempt to revoke these trusts through court proceedings. Hopefully, they will consider all the advantages and protection trusts provide before they charge off to court.

In addition to the changes in the Estate and Gift tax laws, the new law includes reductions in individual income tax rates, modifications to the child tax credit, elimination of the so called marriage penalty tax, expansion of the adoption credit provisions, increased contributions to education IRA accounts, modification of IRA contribution limits with catch up provisions for individuals over age fifty, and provisions for expanded coverage for qualified plans including increases in contribution and benefit limits. A brief summary of the changes affecting the estate tax area are as follows.

## Phase Out of Estate and Generation-Skipping Transfer Taxes; Increase in Gift Tax Unified Credit Effective Exemption

Appendix C lists the Federal estate and gift tax rates. The new law slowly decreases these rates. In 2002, the estate and gift tax rates above 53 percent and the 5 percent surtax on estates between $10,000,000 and $17,184,000 are repealed. The new tax rates are as follows.

| Year | Highest Estate and Gift Tax Rates |
|------|-----------------------------------|
| 2002 | 50% |
| 2003 | 49% |
| 2004 | 48% |
| 2005 | 47% |
| 2006 | 46% |
| 2007 | 45% |
| 2008 | 45% |
| 2009 | 45% |
| 2010 | Estate tax repealed, top individual tax rate for gift tax only. |

## Unified Credit is Replaced with a Unified Exemption

The Unified Credit, as explained on page 18, is available to every person for taxable transfers by gift or death. In 2002, the Unified Estate and Gift Tax Credit is replaced with a Unified Exemption amount. The Unified Exemption, the amount of property one can transfer tax free, is as follows:

| In the case of estates of decedents dying during: | The property exclusion amount is: |
|---------------------------------------------------|-----------------------------------|
| 2002 | $1,000,000 |
| 2003 | 1,000,000 |
| 2004 | 1,500,000 |
| 2005 | 1,500,000 |
| 2006 | 2,000,000 |
| 2007 | 2,000,000 |
| 2008 | 2,000,000 |
| 2009 | 3,500,000 |

An important point to keep in mind is that the gift tax exclusion amount will increase to $1,000,000 on January 1, 2002, but will not increase after that. So no tax is payable on gifts up to $1,000,000, but gift tax is payable for gifts over $1,000,000. Because the exclusion for estate tax eventually goes to $3,500,000—after which the estate tax is repealed—the effect of this will be to discourage gifts in excess of $1,000,000. The preference will be to have any transfers on excess of $1,000,000 pass through the estate and benefit from the higher exclusion amounts.

## Basis of Property Acquired from a Decedent

In general, when you sell property such as stocks, boats, artwork, etc., you must pay income taxes on any profit. Profit is calculated by subtracting your basis, or what you paid for the property, from the proceeds of the sale. If you inherit property, most of the time your basis is the fair market value on the decedent's date of death. For example, assume I inherited 500 shares of ABC stock from my mother when she died. She paid $1 per share for the stock and on the date of her death the stock had a fair market value of $10 per share. If I immediately sold the stock for its fair market value, I would pay no income taxes on the sale since my basis in the stock of $5,000 equals what I sold the stock for. Starting in 2010, I will assume my mother's $500 basis in the stock unless the executor allocates an increase in basis. If the executor does not allocate an increase in the basis, and I sell the stock for its fair market value of $5000, I will pay tax on the $4,500 profit.

The rules for allowing an increase (step-up) in the basis of the decedent's assets to fair market value on the date of death (or the alternative date if elected) are replaced in 2010 with a *modified carryover basis procedure.* This means some assets will have as their basis what the deceased person paid for them, while other assets—at the discretion of the executor—will have their basis increased. In general, the basis of assets acquired from a decedent will be the lower of cost or fair market value on the date of death with an allowed increase to basis of $1.3 million. The new law allows the executor to select the assets to receive the step-up in basis. This $1.3 million may be increased for the decedent's unused capital loss carry-overs, net operating losses, (items he could not claim on his final income tax return) and certain "built in" losses of the decedent. Spouses will be allowed to increase the basis of assets received by $3 million. Nonresidents who are not U. S. citizens will be allowed to increase the basis of property by up to $60,000. The allowed basis increases will be adjusted annually for inflation occurring after 2010.

Property will be eligible for the modified basis rules if it is:
1) Acquired by bequest, devise, or inheritance
2) Property acquired by the decedent's estate from the decedent
   1. Property transferred by the decedent in trust where the trust pays all of the income to decedent during his lifetime and the decedent has the right to revoke the trust during his lifetime (living trusts as described in chapter 5)
   2. Property transferred by the decedent in trust during his lifetime to pay the income for life to or on the order or direction of the decedent with the right reserved to the decedent at all times prior to his death to make any change to the enjoyment thereof through the exercise of a power to alter, amend, or terminate the trust
   3. Property passing from the decedent to the extent the property passed without consideration such as joint tenancy and tenants by the entireties (pages 7 and 8)
3) The surviving spouse's one-half share of certain community property held by the decedent and the surviving spouse as community property

Property that will not be eligible for a basis increase includes:
1) Property that the decedent acquired by gift, other than from his or her spouse, during the three year period ending on the date of decedent's death
2) Property that constitutes a right to receive income in respect of a decedent (page 92);
3) Stock or securities of a foreign personal holding company
4) Stock of a current or former Domestic International Sales Corporation
5) Stock of a foreign investment company
   1. Stock of a foreign investment company, except if the decedent shareholder had made a qualifying fund election

# Generation Skipping Transfers

## AUTOMATIC ALLOCATION OF GST EXEMPTION AMOUNT

The objective of estate taxes from the government's point of view is to assess the tax at each generation. One way parents could avoid having their children pay estate taxes would be to leave all of their property to their grandchildren, skipping a generation. Congress recognized this loophole many years ago and passed the Generation Skipping Tax (GST). If a couple leaves all of their property to their grandchildren to avoid having their own children pay estate taxes, the couple will end up paying both their own estate taxes with GST paid by their beneficiaries or trustees when a triggering event occurs as described on page 132. As discussed on page 107, each person may transfer to a person more than one generation below him up to $1,060,000 (2001 amount indexed for inflation) before incurring the GST. The $1,060,000 may be allocated to different transfers. The GST is a flat rate equal to the maximum estate and gift tax rate in effect at the time of the transfer multiplied by what is called the *inclusion ratio*. The inclusion ratio is the number one minus the amount of transferred property subject to the exemption allocation divided by all of the property transferred. So, if $2,000,000 is transferred, the inclusion ratio is 1- (1,060,000–2,000,000) = .47. The GST tax rate is then .47 multiplied by the highest estate tax rate (55%) = .2585. The allocation reduces the amount of the GST.

The new law provides for an automatic allocation of the GST exemption to transfers that are indirect skips. Previously, as stated on page 19, if the decedent failed to allocate his $1,060,000 exemption, it was lost forever. An individual can elect not to have the automatic allocation rules apply by making the election on a timely filed gift tax return for the calendar year the gift was made.

## RETROACTIVE ALLOCATION OF GST EXEMPTION

As described on page 132, GST may be due if a taxable termination occurs by death, lapse of time, or release of a power of an interest in property unless at no time may any distribution be made to a skip person (grandchild). For example, a grandfather may have transferred $1,060,000 in a trust for his son with his son's children as contingent beneficiaries. Because his son is not two generations below him, no GST would be due. However, if the son dies prior to his father and the grandchildren are now the beneficiaries, GST may be due. The new law eliminates this by providing that if a lineal descendant (child) of the decedent dies before the decedent, the decedent (executor obviously) may retroactively allocate GST exemption amount to the trust. In order to make the retroactive allocation to the trust, the beneficiary must be 1) a non-skip person, 2) a lineal descendant of the transferor's (decedent's) grandparent or a grandparent of the transferor's spouse, 3) a generation younger than the transferor, and the beneficiary dies before the transferor. The allocation and inclusion ratio are determined based on the value of the property on the date transferred into the trust.

## SEVERING OF TRUSTS
The new law makes it easier to calculate the GST due by providing for the severing of trusts holding property having an inclusion ratio of greater than zero. If a trust is divided in a qualified severance, the resulting trusts shall be considered separate trusts. A qualified severance is when 1) a single trust is divided into two or more trusts and the single trust was divided on a fractional basis, and 2) the terms of the new trusts provide for the same succession of interest of the beneficiaries as provided for in the original trust. If a trust has an inclusion ratio of greater than zero and less than one, a severance will qualify if the single trust is divided into two trusts, one of which receives a fractional share of the total value of all trust assets equal to the applicable fraction of the single trust immediately before the severance. In this case, the trust receiving the fractional share shall have an inclusion ratio of zero and the other trust shall have an inclusion ratio of one.

There are new valuation rules for determining the value of property transferred for purposes of the GST. The value of property transferred in determining the inclusion ratio shall be its gift or estate tax value depending on the circumstances. In the case of a GST exemption allocation made at the conclusion of an inclusion period, the value for determining its inclusion ration shall be its value at that time. The new law also provides relief for making late elections if the GST election was not made on a timely filed gift tax return and substantial compliance with the GST rules for allowing the GST allocation.

# Use of Appreciated Property to Satisfy Pecuniary Bequests
If the executor of the estate uses appreciated property to satisfy a specific bequest, gain will be recognized to the estate only on the difference

between the value on the date of death and the value on the date of the transfer. This rule applies to property held in trust also. The basis for the recipient on such property is the basis in the estate plus any gain recognized.

# Reporting Requirements

## GIFTS

Chapter 11 provides an overview of Gift Tax law. Previously, there were very few Gift Tax Returns (Form 709) filed with the Internal Revenue Service since most gifts are under the annual exclusion amount of $10,000. The new law includes reporting requirements for donors. A donor is required to report to the IRS the basis and character of any non-cash property transferred by gift with a value over $25,000, except for gifts to charitable organizations.

The donor (person making the gift) is required to report to the IRS:
1) The name and taxpayer identification number of the recipient
2) An accurate description of the property
3) The donor's adjusted basis of the property at the time of the gift
4) The donor's holding period
5) Sufficient information to determine if the gain on the sale of the property would be treated as ordinary income
6) Any other information as required by the Treasury Secretary

 Similar information is required to be provided to the recipient.

## TRANSFERS AT DEATH

For transfers at death of noncash assets in excess of $1.3 million and for appreciated property acquired by the decedent within three years of the date of death in excess of $25,000, the executor of the estate or trustee of a revocable trust must report the following to the IRS:
1) The name and taxpayer identification number of the recipient of the property
2) An accurate description of the property
3) The donor's adjusted basis and the fair market value on the date of death
4) The decedent's holding period for the property
5) Sufficient information to determine if the gain on the sale of the property would result in ordinary income

6) The amount of basis increase allocated to the property

7) Any other information as required by the Treasury Secretary

# Recapture of Estate Tax Benefits after Repeal of the Estate Tax

Prior to December 31, 2010, estates may claim certain benefits listed below to reduce their tax liability. If certain requirements are not met, the estate tax savings must be repaid even after the estate tax is repealed.

## QUALIFIED CONSERVATION EASEMENTS

An executor can elect to exclude from the taxable estate up to 40 percent of the value of land subject to a Qualified Conservation Easement subject to certain maximums. If a donor retained development rights in property in the conveyance of a conservation easement that qualified for the estate tax exclusion prior to December 31, 2010, the beneficiaries must enter into an agreement to extinguish development rights prior to the earlier of 1) two years after the decedent's death, or 2) prior to the sale of the land. This provision is retained after the repeal of the estate tax law, and if an agreement is not entered into, the beneficiaries will be liable for the tax savings of the estate. The new law also expanded the location of the property allowable for a qualified conservation easement to any land located in the U. S. and any possession of the U. S.

## SPECIAL USE VALUATION

If a decedent's property qualified for reduced estate taxes due to Special Use Valuation, and a disqualifying event occurs, such as the property ceases to be used for the qualified use within 10 years, after the decedent's death, the estate tax savings must be recaptured. This provision is in effect even after repeal of the estate tax law on December 31, 2010.

## QUALIFIED FAMILY-OWNED BUSINESS DEDUCTION

The Qualified Family-Owned Business Deduction does not apply to the estates of decedents dying after December 31, 2003. If a decedent's property qualified for the Qualified Family-Owned business, and a disqualifying event occurs, such as an heir ceases to use the property for the qualified use within 10 years after decedent's death, the estate tax savings must be recaptured. This provision is in effect even after repeal of the estate tax law on December 31, 2010.

# Gain on the Sale of the Decedent's Principal Residence

The current income tax exclusion of $250,000 of the gain on the sale of a principal residence that has been used by the owner as a principal residence in 2 out of the 5 preceding years is extended to estates and heirs by the new law. If an heir uses the residence as their principal residence, the decedent's period of ownership and occupancy can be added to the heir's ownership and occupancy in determining if the $250,000 exclusion applies.

# State Death Tax Credits

Every estate is allowed a credit against the estate tax for state death taxes. The new law reduces the credit from the current amounts 25 percent in 2002, 50 percent in 2003, and 75 percent in 2004. In 2005, the credit is repealed and estates will be allowed to deduct the entire amount of state death taxes paid.

# Penalties for Failure to File Required Returns

## GIFTS

Any donor required to report a gift to the IRS is subject to a penalty of $500 for each failure to report and a penalty of $50 for each failure to report information to the donee.

## TRANSFERS AT DEATH

Any person required to report at death noncash assets in excess of $1.3 million who fails to do so is liable for a penalty of $10,000 for the failure to report such information. Any person required to report appreciated property with a value in excess of $25,000 received by the decedent within 3 years of the date of death who fails to report is liable for a penalty of $500 for such failure to report to the IRS. There is also a penalty of $50 for each failure to report required information to a beneficiary.

.    No penalties are imposed if the failure to report is due to reasonable cause. If the failure to report is an intentional disregard of the rules, the penalty is 5 percent of the fair market value of the property for which reporting was required determined as of either the date of death or the date of making of the gift.

## Additional New Tax Provisions

The Education Individual Retirement Account contribution limit is increased from $500 to $2,000 per year. The withdrawals are tax free if used for educational expenses. The new law provides that an individual is allowed as an itemized deduction the cost of qualified tuition and related expenses up to certain maximums based on their adjusted gross income. The limit on Individual Retirement Account contributions of $2,000 is replaced with the following limits:

| For taxable years beginning in: | The deductible amount is: |
| --- | --- |
| 2002 through 2004 | $3,000 |
| 2005 through 2007 | 4,000 |
| 2008 and later | 5,000 (to be increased by cost of living index) |

In the case of an individual age 50 before the close of the taxable year, the deductible amount is increased by an applicable amount as follows:

| For taxable years beginning in: | The applicable amount is: |
| --- | --- |
| 2002 through 2005 | $ 500 |
| 2006 and later | 1,000 |

# Foreword

I first became interested in the field of estate planning while employed by the Internal Revenue Service. I read various books on estate planning and attended free seminars sponsored by a range of organizations. It seemed most estate planners were concerned with: (1) helping me avoid probate with living trusts; (2) sheltering $1,350,000 in property from estate taxation (which I do not have); or (3) wanting me to become their client and invest in mutual funds and buy insurance. While these are significant issues, they are not the only issues in estate planning.

After leaving the Internal Revenue Service, I began assisting executors and administrators with estates. I found there were few, if any, books that I could recommend to guide them through the process. Similar books are too detailed to comprehend in the short time frame allowed or too general to be of any real assistance.

Although this book often cites Illinois law, many state laws are similar. Since there are variations in each state, and laws are constantly changing, the reader is advised to check with an attorney familiar with her state's laws prior to drafting an estate plan or administering an estate. Also, while the federal laws discussed in this book are applicable to each state, some federal laws rely upon the property law of that particular state in their calculations and interpretations, especially community property states. For example, the Medicaid laws and regulations, although based on federal law, will vary from state to state, since each state administers the program subject to the federal guidelines.

Each person is advised to seek the advice of a competent estate-planning attorney for his specific needs. (In writing this book, I treat the terms "he" and "she" interchangeably.) It is reader's responsibility to make sure the facts and laws discussed in this book are applicable to his situation. I hope readers understand that each topic discussed could have its own book. Hopefully, this book will give users a sufficient awareness and general understanding of the issues involved to ask the right questions of their attorneys or other professional advisors.

—EDMUND T. FLEMING

# Key to Sources Cited

This text refers to many IRS publications, which you may want to access. Use this key to find out what type of publication is cited and where it can be found. Remember also that IRS information (and forms) can be found at *www.irs.gov*.

IRC  INTERNAL REVENUE CODE TITLE 26
This is the federal income and estate tax code, available at most libraries.

CFR  CODE OF FEDERAL REGULATIONS
These are laws promulgated by agencies within their authority, available at most libraries.

PLR  PRIVATE LETTER RULING
This is advice given by the IRS to a taxpayer on a given set of facts. A PLR may not be cited as precedent, but gives taxpayers an idea of how the IRS views a particular set of facts. It is available on Lexis, also Commerce Clearing House *IRS Letter Rulings Reporter*.

TAM  TECHNICAL ADVICE MEMORANDUM
This is advice given by the IRS national office to their revenue agents pertaining to a given set of facts. Available on Lexis, and also Commerce Clearing House *IRS Letter Rulings Reporter*.

REV. PROC.  REVENUE PROCEDURE
This is a procedure issued by the IRS national office. It is available in libraries that carry the IRS cumulative bulletin.

REV. RUL.  REVENUE RULING
This is a ruling on a given set of facts by the IRS national office. Also available in libraries that carry IRS cumulative bulletin.

# Introduction to Estate Planning and Administration

Estate planning is decision making. The process can be relatively simple or quite complex, depending on many factors. Most of us put off any estate planning until we see friends and close relatives pass away, or read horror stories about someone who lost his life savings through fraud. In general, the process involves: (1) choosing how your future health-care decisions will be made when and if you are unable to make informed decisions; (2) deciding how you want your property distributed upon your death; and (3) reviewing your future income and expenses. With inflation, changes in family structure, and new laws passed each year, you should review your estate plan at least once a year. This book includes steps you may follow in drafting and reviewing your plan.

Estate administration is the process of winding up a person's affairs at death. It is the *executor*'s responsibility to ensure that the *will* provisions are followed. It is the *trustee*'s responsibility to ensure that the trust agreement provisions are followed. There are factors for executors and trustees to consider, and many pitfalls to avoid. In estates with *testamentary trusts,* there is usually the question of funding the trusts. The administration of an estate can be simple if the *decedent* left everything he owned in *joint tenancy* or *living trusts,* or complex if there are issues involving *probate* courts, property located in different states, or the filing of complex tax returns. If a *beneficiary* contests the interpretation of a will or trust document, this will increase the amount of time it takes to close the estate. This book provides checklists for those involved in the administration of an estate.

Hopefully, by the time you have read (at least skimmed) this book, you will have decided that, as a minimum, you need a will, *power of attorney* for property, and a health-care directive. If you feel that you don't have the time or money for estate planning, consider the following situations.

EXAMPLE #1      This past holiday season I met a couple in their early fifties. Recently, the husband became ill and fell into a coma. The wife does not have a power of attorney for her husband and therefore cannot sign his name to checks and bills. If his condition does not improve, she may have to become his court-appointed *guardian.* Had the couple taken the time to *execute* durable powers of attorney, they would not be facing expensive attorney fees.

EXAMPLE #2      The wife of a man in his late forties passed away leaving behind two children. The man remarried and then died himself without changing his will. The second wife now owns all of the property and it is doubtful the man's two children (who are not *minors*) will receive any of their parent's property. (The man should have drafted a will with a *qualified terminal interest property (QTIP) trust*—explained later—which would provide income for his new spouse for her life but leave his property to his children.)

EXAMPLE #3      A friend told me about a case involving a widow who died leaving a will that named a trust as a beneficiary. No one can locate the trust agreement. The attorney fees and litigation concerning the lost agreement will cut significantly into the estate, leaving little, if any, for the beneficiaries. If the widow had followed the checklists contained in this book, she could have either located the trust agreement or made other arrangements to eliminate the future confusion.

EXAMPLE #4      A woman in her eighties who was receiving Medicaid assistance was named beneficiary in her sister's will. When the sister died, the woman tried to disclaim her inheritance so as not to affect her Medicaid benefits, but was unable to disclaim the inheritance. If proper estate planning had taken place, nieces and nephews would have been named as beneficiaries instead. This lack of estate planning cost her approximately $50,000.

EXAMPLE #5     A mother decided she wanted to avoid probate at all costs and felt the easiest way to do this was place her son's name on all of her property, including her home. She knew that property held in joint tenancy goes to the other joint tenants upon the death of a joint tenant. She had to move into an apartment when her son's creditors forced a sale of the house.

EXAMPLE #6     A decedent executed a living trust agreement in 1990. He then executed a series of amendments to his trust agreement starting in 1991. By mistake, he executed two second amendments to the trust agreement one year apart. The beneficiaries are now in court trying to decide on the correct interpretation of the trust amendments.

## Who Needs Estate Planning?

While I admit that one of the above situations is fictional, I hope you see the benefits of estate planning. Individuals who should have an awareness of different aspects of estate planning include just about everyone. If you have minor children, you should be concerned with naming guardians to take care of them, and need to execute a will to nominate guardians. If you have an item of property you would like to leave to a particular person, besides giving it to her immediately or carving her initials on it, you should execute a will or place the item in a trust for her future enjoyment. If you are named as an *executor* in a will, agent on a power of attorney, or trustee of a trust agreement, you will need an overview of your authority and responsibilities. If you have advanced money to one child so he could buy a house but want your children to inherit equally, you should mention in your will if the loan needs to be repaid; otherwise your children will be left wondering if the advance was really a *gift* or a loan.

*Estate Planning and Administration* will give you an overview of the issues that you may meet in this many-faceted area. Most importantly, it should provide you with the ability to ask the right questions of your attorney, accountant, certified financial planner, and insurance agent either in planning your own estate or when acting as an executor or trustee.

# 2

# The Planning Process

Planning your personal and financial affairs is a benefit both to yourself and your family. Estate planning can be relatively simple and straightforward, or complex and time-consuming. Everyone has different goals in life. The same is true for estate planning. Once you have assembled the key documents and reviewed your current financial affairs, you should select the goals or objectives that are most important to you. Prioritize your objectives, so your advisors will know which options are available to you.

Take extra time and use caution when choosing an executor, trustee, or agent on a power of attorney. The individuals best suited for these offices are responsible, mature, have the time to assume the duties, and are trustworthy. You should decide who will make health-care and financial decisions for you if there comes a time when you cannot make your own decisions. In addition, if there are individuals dependent upon you, such as minor children or aged parents, proper planning today may save thousands of dollars in accounting and legal fees at a later date.

Everyone has different priorities and concerns, based on his situation in life and personal beliefs. When reviewing your estate planning, you may find that caring for your parents is your highest priority. Your neighbors, whose parents have passed away, may be more concerned with probate or tax avoidance. A sample of goals to consider include estate-tax avoidance, income-tax issues (including current income-tax issues, income and deductions in respect of a decedent, and future beneficiary income taxes), avoidance of probate, preservation of accumulated wealth, asset protection, long-term health care, the selection of agents on durable powers of attorney, medical directives, guardians for minor children, care for disabled adults, charitable intentions, and business succession.

## Points to Consider

- Many people put off estate planning because they believe it only involves saving taxes or avoiding probate. Estate planning also involves your future financial and health affairs, guardians for minors, asset protection, and various other issues.
- Estate planning is for everyone, not just the wealthy.
- Do not be fooled into thinking that a fully funded revocable trust (living trust) will solve all of your estate concerns.
- Select attorneys, accountants, and insurance agents who take the time to listen to your needs and charge reasonable prices for their services.

The steps listed below should be followed in planning your financial and health-care future.

1. Identify Your Property
2. Establish Objectives
3. Select Your Advisors
4. Draft and Implement a Plan
5. Perform an Annual Review

## Step 1: Identify Your Property

You need to know your current situation before you can begin the estate-planning process. How you hold title to property will affect how it can be transferred, if at all. The best-drafted will cannot transfer property to your sister if you hold title in joint tenancy with your brother-in-law. If you live in a *community-property* state (I am very thankful Illinois is not a community-property state), such as Arizona, California, Idaho, Louisiana, Nevada, New Mexico, Texas, Washington, and Wisconsin (partial), you should find a local estate-planning attorney well versed in that state's rules concerning *community property.* Taking the time to ask for copies of *beneficiary designation forms* from IRA trustees and *payable-on-death desig-*

*nation forms* from your bank may show you that property is to be distributed to beneficiaries other than how you remembered. Review any existing trust agreements that are in place. Do you have complete *power of appointment* over the property? If yes, it will be included in your estate.

## HOW DO YOU HOLD TITLE TO PROPERTY?

There are advantages and disadvantages involved in how you hold title to property, for example, in regard to *creditor protection laws.* Check with your attorney and accountant prior to transferring any interest in property. It may be that you should not transfer ownership of certain property. If you gift a partnership interest to your son, you may trigger taxable income to yourself depending on your basis and partnership liabilities. If you transfer ownership of your residence to your daughter, you may lose the benefits of a homeowner's real-estate tax exemption and trigger an acceleration clauses in a mortgage. Property is generally held by one of the following methods, not considering *adverse possession, easements, life estates,* powers of appointment, *remainder* and *reversionary interests,* and some other minor forms of ownership.

### COMMUNITY PROPERTY

This is property accumulated during a marriage, unless received by gift or inheritance, in the states of Arizona, California, Idaho, Louisiana, Nevada, New Mexico, Texas, Washington, and Wisconsin

### FEE SIMPLE ABSOLUTE

This means the owner has absolute ownership of a piece of property. This is the highest form of ownership. Title may be shown as "John Smith."

### JOINT TENANCY

This is a form of ownership whereby each person acquired his interest at the same time, in the same amount, by the same deed, and have present possession. The deed must state it is joint tenancy or it will be considered tenancy in common (see below). At a joint tenant's death, his interest passes to the surviving joint tenants (technically, the interest is extinguished). Title may be shown as "John Smith and Mary Jones as Joint Tenants."

### JOINT TENANCY WITH RIGHT OF SURVIVORSHIP

This is a form of ownership for married couples only. When one spouse dies, his interest is extinguished and the other owns 100 percent of the property. Title may be shown as "John Smith and Mary Smith, Husband and Wife, as Joint Tenants with Right of Survivorship."

### TENANCY BY THE ENTIRETY

This is a form of ownership created by a married couple. Since neither spouse may encumber the property without the consent of the other, this form of ownership is superior for creditor protection and should be considered by individuals who may be subject to lawsuits, such as doctors and lawyers. Tenancy by entirety includes the right of survivorship. Some states do not allow this form of ownership and, if title is held this way, will consider this as joint tenancy. Title should be shown as "John Smith and Mary Smith, Husband and Wife, as Tenants by the Entireties, and not as Joint Tenants or as Tenants in Common."

### TENANCY IN COMMON

This is ownership of a piece of property by two or more persons (who may or may not be married) and either the deed does not state it is held in joint tenancy, or the parties do not meet one of the requirements for joint tenancy. This form of ownership does not include the right of survivorship; when an owner dies, his interest passes to his *heirs,* not the other tenants. Title may be shown as "John Smith and Mary Jones."

## TRUSTS

A trust is an equitable form of ownership. All property has both a *legal title* and *equitable title.* A trustee holds the legal title to a piece of property while the beneficiary holds equitable title. There are many formats and uses for trusts in estate planning—you must be careful to draft a trust agreement that will meet your needs. Title may be shown as "John Smith, not individually, but as Trustee of Trust Number 123 dated January 15, 1998."

### CUSTODIAN ACCOUNTS

If the owner of the property is a minor, title to the account will be shown with the custodian's name followed by the minor. This will include transfers of property under *Uniform Gifts or Transfers to Minor's Acts.* Title may be shown as "John Smith, custodian, Therese Smith UGMA, Illinois."

### PAYABLE-ON-DEATH (POD) ACCOUNTS

This is a method of transferring funds used by banks. The owner of the account names a beneficiary to receive the balance of the account upon the death of the owner. The account belongs 100 percent to the owner of the account who may spend the funds as she wishes. The account will not have to go through probate upon the death of the owner, but will belong to the named beneficiary. The account is included in the owner's estate.

### TRANSFER-ON-DEATH DESIGNATIONS

In most states, it is possible to complete forms that will transfer government securities and stocks and bonds upon your death. Check with your broker about filling out the designation forms. This method will help to avoid probate but the amount will be included in your estate.

## ASSEMBLE YOUR KEY DOCUMENTS

The best way to analyze your current financial condition is to assemble all of your key documents in one place. The time you spend today assembling and organizing your financial affairs will save your executor or *administrator* countless time and headaches in the future, and may prevent assets from passing to the state *(escheat)* as when a rightful heir cannot be found. Many people assume incorrectly that their executor will know where they did their banking, where the safe-deposit-box key is hidden, which insurance companies, fraternal organizations, credit unions, and pension plans should be contacted. Complete the background information checklists to assist your executor and update your files on a regular basis.

Assemble the following financial and legal documents in one location, possibly an inexpensive watertight plastic box you can buy at department stores. Make sure the box is large enough to hold legal-size manila folders, which you can then separate into the following sections. Label the folders so you can readily pull out old documents and replace with new information.

### ADMINISTRATION FILE

- Final instructions. Include any instructions you have concerning burial arrangements and services. Include copies of any prepaid funeral arrangements, and deeds and locations to cemetery plots. Also, include any special requests, such as memorial in lieu of flowers, or songs, or prayers.
- Letter of instruction. This is a letter, in your own handwriting, to your executor, guardian, or trustee, which describes your intentions and thoughts with regard to items not included in your will. This may include the distribution of personal items not specifical-

ly bequeathed in the will and/or a list of charities you would like to have your artwork or personal items, such as clothes, furniture, etc., if no one claims these items. Letters of instruction are not legally binding, but generally will be followed by your loved ones.

- Safe-deposit-box keys. Write the location of the safe-deposit-box keys, and name and address of the box location. Keep the safe-deposit-box agreement in the same folder.

### BUSINESS FILE
- Buy/sell agreements with *closely held companies*
- Corporate stock certificates for closely held companies
- Deferred compensation plan statements and brochures
- Financial statements of the business
- Installment contracts on sales of property
- Key employee life-insurance policies
- Partnership agreements
- Rental documents, such as leases and records of deposits
- Stock-redemption agreements

### FINANCIAL FILE
- Appraisals of property (jewelry, homes, antiques, collectibles)
- Insurance policies: burial, disability, life, long-term care, medical
- List of all your account numbers: checking, savings, *land trusts*
- Monthly account statements from brokers
- Monthly checking-account statements
- Purchase invoices of large-ticket items, such as cars and jewelry
- Savings passbooks and loan documents
- Stock certificates (if not in the safe-deposit box)
- U.S. savings bonds (if not in the safe-deposit box)

### LEGAL FILE
- *Anatomical gift* declarations (organ donations)
- Deeds to real estate with title policies
- Executory contracts: These are agreements that are not fully completed, such as an agreement with an attorney to handle a lawsuit, or a contractor to build a house.

- Medical directives, *health-care power of attorney,* and *living will*
- Powers of attorney for property
- Trust agreements and amendments
- Will and *codicils* (yours). You should have a copy of your latest will and any amendments (codicils). Have a note about where the original can be located. Do not write on the copy, in case the original cannot be found.
- Will and codicils (spouse's, even if the spouse is deceased)

PERSONAL FILE
- Adoption certificates
- Birth certificates
- Divorce agreements (to protect against false *claims*)
- Marriage certificates
- Military discharge papers (for funeral allowance and flag)
- Prenuptial agreements

PROPERTY AND DEBT FILE
- Car, truck, boat, and trailer titles, registration, and insurance policies
- Loan agreements and payoff letters
- Mortgages and payment books
- Warranty brochures
- Appraisals for expensive property

TAX RETURN FILE
- Federal and state income-tax returns. While the statute of limitations is generally three years for income-tax returns, it may prove helpful in tracing assets if you retain returns for at least the past five years.
- *Gift tax* returns (Form 709)
- Trust and *fiduciary* returns (Form 1041)
- Estate-tax returns (Form 706). If you have inherited any property in the last ten years (or a decedent inherits property within two years of date of death), retain copies of returns filed for a credit on the federal estate-tax return.

## Step 2: Establish Objectives

Once you have assembled and reviewed your key documents, you can begin the second step in the process, which is to determine what your goals and objectives are with regards to your person, property, and income. You can have numerous goals, but select one or two as your highest priorities. Your objectives may change over time. The priorities you select today could be the care of your minor children and business succession. Ten years from now your main objectives may be the avoidance of probate and saving estate taxes. If you review your plan once each year, you can adjust your financial affairs to fit your objectives.

Most of the estate-planning techniques, such as the *unlimited marital deduction* and QTIP trust, seem to benefit married couples rather than single persons or unmarried couples. There are techniques that should be considered by unmarried couples, such as the *bypass trust,* which will allow the decedent to care for a partner for life and then direct the transfer of property to beneficiaries upon the death of the partner.

### PERSONAL OBJECTIVES

#### FUTURE FINANCIAL DECISION-MAKING

There are three basic methods through which your future financial decision-making will occur if you are unable to make decisions.

1. *Agent with a power of attorney for property.* Executing a power of attorney naming your spouse, child, or close friend is the easiest and least expensive method to grant a person the ability to make decisions for you when you are unable to do so for health reasons. The agent does not have to be an attorney, but please remember: You are granting one individual an enormous amount of responsibility and authority with no supervision. You should always name a successor agent in case the first agent can no longer act.

2. *Guardian appointed by a court.* This may be *limited, temporary,* or *plenary guardianship.* The guardian must provide accountings to the court, so there will be loss of privacy. The individual can contest the guardianship and could demand a jury trial. The benefits of guardianship over other methods are supervision and protection.

3. *Trustee named in a trust agreement.* This may be the best method for long-term care of an individual, since a trustee has a lawful duty to act, whereas an individual with a power of attorney has no duty to act. A trustee has certain fiduciary responsibilities that an agent on a power of attorney does not have. Consider providing for compensation for the trustee if this is a family member who will do the work.

### HEALTH-CARE DECISIONS

You can execute both a health-care power of attorney and a living will. Statutory health-care powers of attorney adopted in certain states allow an individual to make health-care decisions for the principal, and grant powers, such as the ability to request an autopsy and review medical records. The principal can limit the powers granted to the agent by crossing out the powers on the document. A living will is a medical directive to the doctor with no agent involved.

### CARE FOR MINOR CHILDREN

If you have minor children, generally under the age of eighteen, you should execute a will that names a guardian for their welfare and a trustee of a minor's trust for their financial concerns. The trust language can be included in the same document as the will. Try not to name married couples as beneficiaries, executors, trustees, or guardians, since there are many divorces. When selecting a guardian for your children, remember that you are not required to ask that person in advance if she would be willing to act as guardian, although you can if you wish. If you later have a falling out with that person, you may change your mind. Selecting a guardian is a very difficult decision. You can address a letter, often called a letter of instruction, in your own handwriting to the guardian describing your wishes as to how your child should be raised. Your intentions may be followed by the guardian and trustee, although this is not a legally enforceable document.

### CARE FOR ELDERLY PARENTS

If you are caring for your parents, as more and more individuals are, consider establishing a living trust for their benefit with a *corporate successor trustee,* should anything happen to you. If they currently live at home while you live in another state, there are companies you can contract, which will check on their welfare. If long-term care is needed, you can contact your state agency that regulates nursing homes and ask for brochures on regulations and listings of homes. Contact nursing homes for a description of services provided, a listing of activities, financial and health requirements, placement availability, and a copy of the contract.

If you hire a "live-in" to care for your parents, check with your insurance agent to make sure the homeowner policy covers the caregiver. The policy may not cover her, since she is neither a guest nor resident of the home. You may have to purchase an insurance rider, but the nominal fee will prove worthwhile if the caregiver has an accident in the home.

### CARE FOR DISABLED CHILD OR ADULT WITH SPECIAL NEEDS

Establish a *supplemental security income (SSI) trust* to supplement government entitlement programs and provide long-term security. An SSI trust or a *special needs trust* must be carefully drafted to ensure the beneficiary is not cut off from government entitlements. Check to make sure the person is not the direct beneficiary in your will, which may result in a loss of funding due to the inheritance; name the SSI trust itself the direct beneficiary. This is an irrevocable trust, which will require separate records and a trustee, but the benefits will be more than the costs to establish.

### PROTECTING THE INTERESTS OF CHILDREN FROM A FIRST MARRIAGE

Establish a QTIP trust if you have children from a first marriage so that you can care for your current spouse for her life but ensure that your property goes to your children upon her death. While you may be correct in your assumption that your second spouse will care for your children, many things can happen, such as death or remarriage. Protect your children with a valid QTIP trust. Property that passes into the QTIP qualifies for the unlimited marital deduction for tax deferral but will be included in the spouse's estate when she dies. Both personal and real property can be placed into the QTIP trust. Some individuals have more than one QTIP trust. They establish one QTIP trust during their lifetime and have a testamentary QTIP established through their will. However, there are expenses involved with drafting the QTIP, and you may be tying up property in a trust for many years. If you are concerned with paying the least amount of federal estate taxes, in addition to providing for your children, you may consider drafting a *credit shelter trust* first and retain a sufficient amount of property in your own name or fund the credit shelter trust. The remainder of your property can then be placed into the QTIP trust.

## PROPERTY OBJECTIVES

### ASSET PROTECTION

In today's world, countless lawsuits are filed. Some may appear frivolous, but if you are the defendant, it is always serious business. Some means of protecting property include transferring ownership to offshore accounts, such as in the Bahamas or Cayman Islands, where the assets will be hard for creditors to reach. You can execute irrevocable trusts, which will take the property out of your name and control. Certain states now allow trusts to exist for long periods of time without regard to the *rule against perpetuities.* Delaware, Alaska, and other states allow so-called *dynasty trusts,* which can be used to provide for future generations of your *descendants* without the property being included in each generation's taxable estates. There are requirements—for example, part of the trust must be kept in the state—but in this day of electronic commerce, this should be easy to comply with. The dynasty trust has all the advantages of irrevocable trusts, such as privacy, probate avoidance, incapacity planning, and protection for assets, but it also is a means of building wealth for future generations. These trusts should only be used with significant amounts of wealth, since in future generations there may be many beneficiaries, and the costs of handling the trust may exceed the intended benefits. You also cannot use offshore trusts to hide your assets if you retain control over the trustee. One court recently held a couple in contempt of court for not turning over funds held in an offshore account.

### AVOID DISSENTION BETWEEN YOUR BENEFICIARIES

Write a letter of instruction concerning the distribution of personal property not listed in your will, make your own prearranged funeral arrangements, and discuss your plans with beneficiaries in advance. It doesn't hurt to ask each person privately if there is something you own she would like to inherit, such as a piece of antique jewelry. If one person has been caring for you for the past several years, running you to the doctor, buying medicines, visiting on weekends and holidays while no one else has visited you in those years, consider leaving this person more than others, since she is more deserving. You can put a clause in your will that says if anyone contests the will he will receive nothing, but this seems a little extreme for most people and may lead to questions of undue influence.

AVOIDING PROBATE

Avoiding probate is not as important in most states as it once was. Many states have procedures for *independent administration,* which lower the costs of probate. There are definite advantages to going through probate, and chapter 7 provides a more detailed look at the advantages and disadvantages of probate. Probably the main advantage for going through probate is that it provides for a six-month creditor cutoff period. Without probate, a large, unexpected bill could show up two years after the deceased had passed away, leaving the heirs discussing who should pay the bill. Probate provides finality to the costs of an estate.

However, if you wish to avoid probate, establish a living trust and transfer most, if not all, of your property into the trust. In general, keep personal property not in the living trust to $50,000 or less, so that a *small-estate affidavit* can be used in lieu of probate to transfer assets. Check for the small-estate procedures for your state. You can avoid probate and possibly reduce your estate-tax burden by placing your residence or vacation home in a *Qualified Personal Residence Trust (QPRT).* Check if your state allows land trusts for your personal residence. Remember that everyone should have a will in addition to any living trust or other trust. Keeping ownership of all your property in joint tenancy to avoid probate is not recommended for anyone due to loss of *stepped-up basis,* potential creditor issues, and loss of the *unified credit.* (When you own property in joint tenancy and pass away, your interest is extinguished; the surviving joint tenant now owns your interest. In order for your beneficiaries to take advantage of your unified-credit amount, the property must be held in your name alone.) You can use payable-on-death designations for bank accounts and securities, which will keep the property out of probate but not save on estate taxes.

CHARITABLE INTENTIONS

If you are in a relatively secure financial position and intend to leave money or property to a charity, you may wish to establish a *charitable trust.* This may result in current income tax deductions but the property is forever out of your control, since this is an irrevocable trust. The current tax savings may enable you to pay premiums on term life-insurance policies to replace some of the lost wealth for your beneficiaries.

You can designate a charity as beneficiary on a life-insurance policy that you transfer to an irrevocable trust. The premiums are deducted currently as a charitable donation. You can also donate the remainder interest in your house or other property to a charity by deed. Within certain time frames, you are able to donate appreciated stock and claim a charitable deduction for its *fair market value*. In order for you to claim a charitable deduction, the charity must be a qualified organization recognized by the IRS. See IRS publication 78 for a cumulative list of organizations described in §170 (c) of the Internal Revenue Code of 1986, or check with your local IRS office to see if contributions will qualify for a charitable tax deduction.

### CONCERN FOR A BENEFICIARY UNDERGOING A DIVORCE OR FINANCIAL PROBLEMS

If you have a beneficiary who is undergoing financial difficulties, such as pending lawsuits or judgments, a divorce, or is too immature to handle money, establish a *spendthrift trust* for his benefit and leave money directly to the trust (not the individual). This will provide protection from creditors and hopefully provide the individual money to care for himself for a long time in the future.

### CONCERN WITH SPOUSE'S CONTINUED DRIVING

If your spouse will not "give up the keys," and you are concerned that an accident could erase your accumulated wealth, purchase a large umbrella insurance policy and transfer property out of your names. Also, contact (anonymously) the office in charge of driver registration to let your state know that this person should not be driving.

### ELIGIBILITY FOR MEDICAID LONG-TERM CARE

Transfer property thirty-six months (sixty months, if in a trust) prior to completing an application for Medicaid. Establish a Medicaid qualifying trust (although there are significant new restrictions.) There are federal laws against hiding assets to qualify for Medicaid, so make sure you review your situation with a competent attorney familiar with the Medicaid laws.

### EQUITABLE DISTRIBUTION OF PROPERTY BETWEEN YOUR CHILDREN

Check if any loans or advancements made to a child are accounted for in your will. Check that estate taxes will not come out of only one child's share of your estate. Estate taxes generally will not come from any advancements made or assets that pass outside of probate. Make sure that any tax-apportionment language is identical in the will and trust agreements. Check that one beneficiary does not receive all *income-in-respect-of-a-decedent (IRD)* property while another receives non-income-in-respect-of-a-decedent property. For example, one child may receive the balance in your IRA account of $150,000, while a second child receives a vacation house worth $150,000. This seems fair until you realize the first child will end up paying income taxes on the IRA account when withdrawn, while the second child will not pay income taxes on the house.

If you have significant wealth and are leaving money to your grandchildren, allocate your *generation-skipping transfer tax-exemption* fairly between the grandchildren's trusts.

### LEAST AMOUNT OF STRESS FOR YOUR EXECUTOR

Assemble your key financial documents and tell your executor where they are stored. Also, consider providing for a specific dollar amount of compensation to the executor. Although this is not required, it is fair, since one person generally does all the work in wrapping up the affairs. Transfer property into trusts to reduce the amount of probate time and cost required. Make your own funeral arrangements, purchase a cemetery plot, and place the information about these arrangements in your files. Although it sounds difficult to plan your own funeral, it gives you the ability to decide how you would like everything to proceed. Funerals are a difficult enough time for your loved ones without the burden of choosing a casket, prayer cards, flowers, and other items. Write a letter of instruction to the executor to explain your wishes for items not listed in a will or trust.

### PAY THE LEAST AMOUNT OF FEDERAL ESTATE TAXES

Several methods for decreasing the amount of federal estate taxes that your estate may end up paying are discussed in chapter 8. For example, make sure each spouse takes full advantage of his or her unified credit *(exclusion amount)*. Each spouse should have sufficient property in his or her name alone to take full advantage of the credit. If possible, start a gifting program to your beneficiaries when your gross estate is at the exclusion amount. Consider a QPRT, especially if you have a vacation home, to pass the interests in real estate currently to your children and save the appreciation from estate taxes.

Consider a *generation-skipping trust (GST)* in your plans if you have significant accumulated wealth. Each individual may leave up to $1 million to members of a generation one step below their children without the additional GST tax being imposed. The GST tax is in addition to the federal estate and gift taxes. If the GST exemption is not used by a person, it is lost forever. In your will and trust agreements, give the executor and trustee the express authority to allocate the GST exemption if you have not previously made the election. Married couples may elect gift splitting under §2513 of the Internal Revenue Code for a total $2 million GST credit. Provided that both spouses are citizens or residents of the United States, a gift by one spouse to someone other than his spouse may, for purposes of the gift tax, be considered as made by the other spouse. People are considered spouses for purposes of the gift tax, if they were married at the time the gift was made and do not remarry during the remainder of that calendar year. Both spouses must signify consent for the gifts to be considered as made one half by each. However, this consent is not effective if, for example, a husband had previously provided his wife with a general power of appointment in such property.

If you have children who are fifty years of age, and you leave them all of your property, it may grow significantly only to be subject to estate taxes again in several years. Consider leaving the $1 million in a trust for your grandchildren and save the family estate taxes on the appreciation.

There may be situations when the unlimited marital deduction should not be used by the executor when filing estate-tax returns. Although a spouse may leave an unlimited amount of property to his partner without the federal estate tax being imposed, this is a tax-deferral, not a tax-avoidance technique. If both spouses die within a short time of one another, it may be better if each spouse paid estate taxes to take advantage of the graduated rates of tax. If the second spouse dies before the first spouse's estate tax return has been filed, the executor should calculate the tax with and without using the unlimited marital deduction on the first spouse's return.

PROVIDE YOUR EXECUTOR WITH READY CASH TO PAY BILLS

There are many expenses that must be paid soon after a person dies. The funeral expenses and burial costs must be paid within weeks of death. You may wish to purchase a small life-insurance policy on yourself and either transfer ownership to your executor or name her the beneficiary. This will provide your executor with cash to pay funeral, utilities, and other expenses. Federal estate taxes are generally due within nine months of date of death except for a minor exception: when 35 percent of the value of the estate consists of a closely held business. Consider making the executor a joint owner of a small checking account or beneficiary of a payable-on-death account at your bank.

### REPLACING ACCUMULATED WEALTH LOST TO FEDERAL ESTATE TAXES

Consider the advantage of a *second-to-die life-insurance policy*. Since estate taxes can be deferred until the second to die with the unlimited marital deduction, this type of policy can be used to replace the wealth lost to estate taxes. This policy is less expensive than a regular life-insurance policy. Execute an *irrevocable life-insurance trust* or have your children own the policy to keep the proceeds out of your estate.

### SMOOTH TRANSFER OF YOUR BUSINESS TO CHILDREN

If you are operating a sole proprietorship and are concerned with its ability to continue as a going concern upon your death, give your executor the power in your will to continue and manage the business, otherwise the executor only has the power to wrap up business operations. Draft buy/sell agreements with your estate or potential buyers. Have the business purchase key-man life insurance on your life to provide cash to purchase your interest. If you have a closely held business and are not concerned with a stepped-up basis, you may consider transferring the business into a *family partnership*. If you grant an agent the authority on a power of attorney to manage your business, make sure you consider including compensation for the agent for the time and effort involved. Remember that an agent on a power of attorney has no authority once the principal dies.

### TRANSFER OF A SUBCHAPTER S CORPORATION TO YOUR CHILDREN

If you own a Subchapter S corporation that is increasing in value, you may consider the use of a *grantor-retained annuity trust* for transfer to the children. Provided you outlive the term of the trust, you will save significant estate taxes on the transfer. See IRS PLR 9448018. An *Electing Small-Business Trust (ESBT)* may be a shareholder in an Subchapter S corporation. See Notice 97-49, Internal Revenue Bulletin 1997-36.

## INCOME OBJECTIVES

The following are several issues you may discuss with your financial planner. You should consider the amount of income required to maintain your future lifestyle. Will you move to a smaller home with lower real-estate taxes and utilities? Will you be supporting a child and/or parent? Will you be helping your children with college, buying homes, traveling, or starting a business? While certain expenses decrease when you retire, such as commuting expenses and income taxes (since your income is lower), other expenses, such as medical costs, will increase, since your employer will no longer be sharing the insurance premiums. While the subject of investing your money should be handled by a certified financial planner, the decision to transfer property should be made in discussions with your attorney and/or accountant who will know what, when, and how your property should be transferred.

### HEALTH-CARE COSTS

Determine if you can purchase long-term health-care insurance currently through your employer. Contact your insurance agent and ask for an estimate of the cost for such a policy. If you are unable to pay for health care, Medicaid will pay the bills if your income and property are below certain levels. Consider transferring income-producing property to your children now to avoid the Medicaid-prohibited asset transfers. Before you purchase a long-term health-care insurance policy, ask the agent if the premiums paid are tax deductible. Part of the premiums on policies issued after January 1, 1997, are deductible if the policy meets federal guidelines.

### RETIREMENT INCOME

Check with your financial advisor for an estimate of your future income and expenses. Will your pension, social security, deferred compensation accounts, IRA accounts, and other investment income be adequate to maintain your lifestyle? Are you supporting dependents? Should you invest in stock, mutual funds, certificates of deposit, U.S. savings bonds, annuities, or other investments? Your own certified financial planner is the best source of investment advice as opposed to a free seminar or this book. Some tips to consider include the following:

- Diversify your financial holdings. The old saying "don't put all of your eggs in one basket" is very true. If something seems too good to be true, it probably is. The elderly are often the target of fraudulent investment schemes.
- Say "No, thanks" to unsolicited sales pitches. If you receive an unsolicited phone call to buy something, hang up. Never give your charge-card numbers over the phone to someone who says you have won a prize. Never withdraw money from your bank or ATM and give it to someone you don't know, regardless of the reason.

- Read the brochures regarding investments. If a financial advisor is pressing you to invest in one of his funds, ask how he is paid; if he is on a commission for each sale, ask how much of a commission he earns. Is the fund a load or no-load fund (do you have to pay to invest funds)? If there is no front-end load, is there a back-end load (withdrawal charge)? Is the fund insured against loss?

- Check for penalties on early withdrawals from *annuities*. If you are being pressured into buying an annuity, ask if there are penalties if you withdraw money from your annuity for an emergency. Is the annuity for life, term-certain, for your life and your survivor's'? Remember there may be significant tax disadvantages to lump-sum withdrawals, since you will be bunching your income in one tax year.

- Limit your accounts in banks to the FDIC-insured amount. The Federal Deposit Insurance Corporation insures accounts in federally insured institutions up to $100,000 per account category, per person, per bank. If you have $250,000 in a savings account at one bank, only $100,000 of that money is insured against loss by the FDIC. Since there have been recent rule changes, check with your bank regarding insurance coverage of your accounts. You can also check with the FDIC to verify that your bank is federally insured.

- Check for property-tax exemptions. Seniors are often given property-tax exemptions in addition to the regular homeowners exemptions if they have income below certain thresholds. Check with your local taxing authority to see if you are eligible for a tax break, and make sure you file on time. Find out what income level is required to receive the tax break (about $35,000 adjusted gross income) and gift away income-producing property to your beneficiaries to qualify.

- Consider a *reverse mortgage*. If you find that you need additional cash, your children have moved out of the house, and you do not want to move into a smaller home, consider the advantage of a reverse mortgage. This is a procedure whereby you obtain a loan on your house and the bank pays you a monthly amount. The loan is due when you die or move from the house. If you sell your house to your children, they would lose the benefit of the stepped-up basis, since they would not inherit the property. There are high initial costs for a reverse mortgage, since there are the usual loan-closing costs, and lenders have the uncertainty of not knowing when or even if the loan will be repaid. Be careful of fraudulent schemes.

- Check your U.S. savings bonds. Savings bonds stop earning interest after thirty years, except Series E purchased after December 1965. Check if you have bonds purchased in the 1940s, '50s, and '60s. Series E and EE bonds may be rolled over into HH Bonds, tax-free for up to one year after maturity. There are also new I bonds that are indexed to inflation.

- Establish a medical savings account (MSA). If you are self-employed or work for a small employer, contributions to an MSA are tax-deductible subject to limits and distributions. If used for qualified medical expenses, distributions are tax-free. There are penalties for early withdrawals. See Internal Revenue Code §220.

- Establish an *educational individual retirement account.* Beginning January 1, 1998, Internal Revenue Code §530 allows taxpayers to deposit up to $500 into an educational IRA account for a child under age eighteen. Parents, grandparents, friends, and the child may contribute to the account, which will grow tax-free. The child will not pay tax on withdrawals from the account, provided they are for qualified educational expenses.

- Establish a *Roth IRA* account. The Taxpayer Relief Act of 1997 added Internal Revenue Code §408A, which allows an individual to establish a Roth IRA account beginning in 1998. While this account is similar to traditional IRA accounts, contributions to the account are not deductible. The account must be designated as a Roth account when set up. Income earned and qualified distributions from the Roth account are not included in gross income. Be careful of penalties if rolling over other accounts into a Roth account.

- Consider dividend reinvestment plans. Once you have established an account with them, many corporations will allow you to purchase additional shares of stock in small increments without paying brokerage commissions. The dividends can be kept in the account rather than sent to you. This is a sort of forced-savings technique, which many of us can use.

## TRANSFER OF THE FAMILY BUSINESS

If you have sufficient investment income and savings to maintain your desired lifestyle, consider transferring the family business to your children now. There are many advantages and disadvantages to transferring a business prior to your death. If the business is increasing in market value, a transfer will freeze its value for estate-tax purposes. The main disadvantages include asset protection and taxes. Once you transfer ownership of the business, you lose control. Several undesirable events could occur, with the end result being that an unrelated party has partial or complete ownership of the business. A child could go through a divorce with shares of the business transferred as part of a divorce settlement, or declare bankruptcy, or predecease you, leaving the business to a charity named in a will, or sell the business.

If your business is incorporated and you liquidate or sell assets, the business will end up paying taxes on the sales of the assets. If you sell most of the assets, the corporation could end up a Personal Holding Company (PHC), requiring the company to pay Internal Revenue Code §542 PHC tax in addition to the regular corporate income taxes. You need to check with your tax advisor or accountant prior to disposing of business assets.

When your interest is in a partnership, check with your tax accountant prior to transferring your ownership to someone else or to an irrevocable trust. If your share of the partnership liabilities is greater than your basis in the partnership, you may trigger taxable income to yourself on the transfer.

If you enter into a buy/sell agreement with your business, your estate may be able to purchase your shares or interest at a predetermined price. This may help with valuation problems for the estate.

If you have a family-owned business, you are now allowed to exclude up to $1 million from your estate if you meet the requirements under Internal Revenue Code §2033A. There are requirements for number of owners, relationship to decedent, and business usage for ten years. If you have a large business that you plan to leave to your family, review the requirements with your attorney and see if you can qualify. This could result in significant tax savings.

## Step 3: Select Your Advisors

Once you have identified and reviewed your assets and determined what your goals and objectives are, you should find experts to assist in the planning process. You can always contact your local bar association for a referral to an attorney who specializes in estate planning. Even though you may have been pleased with the lawyer who handled your real-estate purchase, if he does not specialize in estate planning, he may do more harm than good. Most professionals associated with estate planning offer free initial consultations. Visit at least two or three experts in each area below and ask questions, such as how long they have been in this field and what professional organizations they belong to. Ask for an estimate of their fees in your case.

## ACCOUNTANT

Your tax accountant will be needed to list and value your property. This is especially true if you have a business. The current value of the business should be appraised to determine its worth for estate-tax purposes. There are different methods of appraising the value of a business, so find an individual who specializes in this field.

## ATTORNEY

An attorney is necessary to draft legal documents such as wills, trusts, deeds, powers of attorney for property and health care, and to provide the latest update on laws and regulations. The attorney will be able to determine how you hold title to property and review existing wills and trust agreements for issues such as powers of appointment. If you intend to hire an attorney, obtain a written contract regarding fees and duties. When hiring an attorney to help you plan your estate, decide in advance who will actually transfer assets into the trusts that are set up. You will save money if you transfer the assets yourself, but you could undermine your own plans if you don't transfer all of the assets. It is also important that everyone understand that the attorney represents your interests, not the beneficiaries, although in certain circumstances the attorney could be found liable to the beneficiaries.

## CERTIFIED FINANCIAL PLANNER

A certified financial planner will be able to provide options for your investment planning after reviewing your goals and current situation. Make sure the advisor provides investment options with various companies and funds rather than one company. Also, inquire as to how the agent will be compensated to ensure he is providing you with the best options, not simply those with the highest financial rewards for himself. If you are retiring from a company and have significant amounts of company stock in a 401(k) plan, determine with your advisor if you should roll over the plan into another deferred compensation plan or pay taxes currently.

## INSURANCE AGENT

An insurance agent can provide you with an estimate for life, health, and property insurance policies. If your gross estate is near the exclusion amount ($675,000 in 2000), you may consider an irrevocable life-insurance trust. Also, consider a small life-insurance policy naming your executor as beneficiary. Second-to-die insurance policies are generally less expensive and will provide ready cash for your executor to administer your estate.

### INVESTMENT BROKER (COMPANY)

Selecting a company that sells a variety of financial products will allow you to diversify your holdings and establish accounts needed in your estate plan. They will be able to establish accounts for the benefit of minors if you wish to start a gifting program to nieces and nephews.

### TRUSTEE

The selection of a person or company to be trustee for irrevocable trusts, successor trustee for living trusts, and trustee for minor's trusts is difficult at best. Banks and investment companies may be the safest but are costly. A trustee must have the time and be responsible. A trustee can legally bind the trust with his actions, so be very careful when choosing a trustee. Do not choose your oldest child to act as trustee (or executor) simply because you do not want to offend them by not selecting them for the position. Select the person who has the time, lives nearby, and is financially responsible. The trustee has fiduciary responsibilities over the trust property.

## Step 4: Draft and Implement a Plan

After you have prioritized your goals, you should draft and implement a plan. All of your planning and decision making will be lost unless you take the time to sign and notarize wills, trusts, powers of attorney, transfer title to property, transfer insurance policies into trusts, notify brokers, make gifts, and follow through with the plan. The plan should state which party is responsible for completing tasks with target dates for completion. For example, you may agree that your attorney is responsible for drafting a living trust agreement in thirty days and you will be the one to transfer stocks into the trust after execution. The following is a list of tasks that may be included in your plan:

- Transfer ownership of insurance policies and other property into the various trusts.

- Sign and notarize wills, durable powers of attorney for health care and property, living wills, and trust agreements.
- Complete gifts by making actual delivery of the property, not a promise to do so in the future. A promissory note is evidence of a loan transaction and does not constitute a valid gift for estate-tax purposes. The *donee* must be aware of the gift for it to be considered a valid gift for tax purposes.
- Instruct your broker to establish accounts under the Uniform Gifts to Minors Act and transfer funds or stocks into these accounts.
- If you have passive-activity-loss property that you intend to transfer, check with your accountant prior to the transfer. Attempt to transfer partnership losses to the beneficiary who can use the losses to offset income taxes.
- If you are a partner in a partnership, check to see if your spouse is the successor in interest for your partnership interest. If not, when you die there could be adverse tax consequences. Attempt to make your spouse a joint owner or successor to your partnership interest.
- If you own U.S. savings bonds in joint ownership with a co-owner who is deceased, go to your bank and apply for new bonds with a new co-owner or name a payable-on-death beneficiary. Check first if the reissuance will have any undesirable tax effects.
- Check to see if your partnership agreement allows an Internal Revenue Code §754 election if you die. This election allows a step up in basis on your share of the partnership property. Many large publicly traded partnerships will not allow the election.
- Write a letter of instruction to your executor or guardian describing any wishes not expressed in your will.

## Step 5: Review Your Estate Plan

Perform a quick review once a year (maybe every tax season) for events that have occurred during the past year that may affect your estate plan.

### ADMINISTRATION FILE

Review your letter of instruction to your executor, and your final instructions. During the past year you may have changed your burial wishes or the final instructions you want your executor to follow. If necessary, replace the instructions with new final instructions.

## BUSINESS FILE

Include new contracts, benefit-plan brochures, rental documents. Do you have partnership interests that were purchased for their tax losses that have now turned into taxable income and should be disposed of? Have there been changes in the stock market or interest rates that will affect your investment strategies? Should you adjust your investment portfolio? If you made specific gifts of stock to each of your children, has one stock doubled in value while the other company has filed for bankruptcy? Consider adjusting the specific gifts to account for changes in values.

## FINANCIAL FILE

Include new insurance policies, claims, and brochures. Check beneficiaries on insurance policies, IRA accounts, and annuities. File change of beneficiary forms if necessary.

## LEGAL FILE

Review will and trust agreements. Are these valid and do they reflect your current intentions? Have there been loans or advances to any beneficiaries that need to be accounted for? Review powers of attorney and health-care directives. Do your agents remain capable of making decisions? Ask your accountant and attorney if there are any new federal or state estate laws that affect your estate plans. If you have an irrevocable life-insurance trust, check to see the trustee has sent the required *Crummey* notices to the beneficiaries.

## PERSONAL FILE

Have there been changes of family members due to marriages, divorces, births of grandchildren, deaths, that need to be taken into consideration? Have the minors named in wills and trust agreements become adults? Have there been any changes in anyone's health or welfare that should be considered in your estate plans? Has any beneficiary applied for Medicaid? If yes, consider changing the beneficiary to the Medicaid-applicant's children, instead of the applicant himself, or else the money will have to be refunded to the state. Have you moved to a new state or acquired property in a different state?

## PROPERTY AND DEBT FILE

Update your inventory listing for acquisitions during the year. Attach any loan-payoff letters to loan agreements, and file new loans.

## TAX RETURN FILE

Add copies of most recently filed federal and state income-tax returns. Generally, you should keep tax returns for three years unless you have carry-forward losses from prior year returns. Keep any gift-tax returns filed.

# 3

# Wills

A will is a written legal document by which a person makes a disposition of his property to take effect upon his death. A will has a number of uses besides transferring property and naming executors and beneficiaries. It can establish trusts, pour-over property into trusts already existing, nominate guardians for your children, waive bonds for executors, and make estate-planning instructions to the executor, such as for QTIP (qualifying terminal interest property) elections. A will generally has no effect on non-*probate property*, such as property held in joint tenancy, or life-insurance policies when beneficiaries are designated. Most wills must be in writing and witnessed. Oral or *nuncupative* wills are allowed only in limited circumstances by a small number of states.

Contingent *bequests* are gifts to the person named if the specified event occurs. For example, if I write in my will that I hereby leave my car to my son Joseph if he survives me, the bequest requires that Joseph survive me in order to receive the car. If Joseph does not survive me, then the gift fails and the car goes back into my estate. If the car is destroyed in an accident and I receive insurance proceeds, Joseph does not receive the insurance proceeds, since cash is not the same as a car.

If you believe that a beneficiary may contest your will, consider placing your property into a trust rather than making gifts by your will. Trusts are not contested as frequently as wills and are more difficult to have declared void by a court.

You are not required to list all of your children in your will. Some people believe that if they wish to disinherit a son or daughter, they must leave the child a gift of at least $1 in their will. This simply is not true. The point of leaving a minimum gift is to prove that the *testator* (maker of the will) knew of the child when executing the will but did not wish to leave him or her anything. This is not required and can just result in more problems for the executor.

Most of the following points to consider are based on the laws typical of many states. Please remember to check with an attorney familiar with your own state's requirements when drafting a will.

## Points to Consider

- In general, a testator (person making the will) must be eighteen years of age and of sound mind and memory in order to execute a valid will. In order to have the testamentary *capacity* to make a will, the testator must have sufficient mental ability to know and remember the people who are the natural objects of his affection, to know the extent and character of his property, and to make a plan of disposition in his mind. It is not necessary that the testator be of absolutely sound mind and memory in every respect. The test for capacity is the testator's ability to know the natural objects of his affection, not knowing them in fact.

- If you have a will drawn up in one state, then move to another state, you should have a lawyer in the new state review your will to ensure it conforms with that state's laws.

- If the will allows the executor to sell real estate, the document must be notarized in addition to being witnessed.

- A living will is not a will, but a declaration that the principal does not want extraordinary life-sustaining measures be taken to prolong his life.

- An attorney who drafts your will may be liable to the beneficiaries if he drafts the will negligently. The attorney owes a duty of care to third parties when he drafts a will.

## General Overview of Wills

A will is a legal document that conforms to the laws of the state where it is executed whereby an individual makes known his desires for the disposition of his property at death. A *holographic will* is a document written in the hand of the testator but not witnessed. Some states do not allow holographic wills under any conditions. Generally, a will must be signed in front of at least two competent witnesses above the age of eighteen who are not beneficiaries or creditors under the will. The witnesses do not have to read the will, they must simply know the testator who is signing his will. A spouse should not be a witness to the other spouse's will. A will is revocable (can be voided or changed) at any time during the testator's lifetime. Most wills contain a *revocation* clause canceling all prior wills and codicils (amendments). A spouse cannot be disinherited in a will in states where spouses can claim a statutory share of marital property. A will can provide for an unequal distribution of property that the heirs would otherwise receive under the state's intestacy (dying without a valid will) laws. A will often directs transfers to trusts. A trust for a minor and the name of the trustee can be established in the same document as the will. Generally, the administrator of an estate must be a U.S. resident, but does not have to be a resident of the state. A guardian nominated for the care of minors needs to be a resident of that state. In a will contest, either party can request a jury trial. Wills can be set aside for undue influence, fraud, mistakes, and other reasons. The executor generally has only the authority to wrap up the business affairs of the decedent. If the testator has a Schedule C business, the will should grant authority to the executor to run the business for a limited time. If a will grants a power of appointment to an individual, that person must be at least eighteen years of age and competent to exercise the power when it is exercised.

## Revocation and Revival

Any discussion about wills, however basic, would not be complete without a brief discussion of revocation and *revival*. Once a person executes a valid will, that legal document can be voided by being physically torn up, obliterated, or burned, or by execution of a new will that contains the language found in all wills: The testator hereby revokes all prior wills and codicils. Once the new will is executed, the prior will (No. 1) is void. What happens if this new will (No. 2) is later determined invalid for some reason? Generally, if a will is determined invalid, the entire document is void. This includes the language revoking prior wills and codicils. Does this mean that will No. 1 is thereby restored to life, or revived? Whether or not will No. 1 has a new life depends on the law of your state and the surrounding facts. This author does not believe a prior will that was once revoked should be given new life unless the second will was made under conditions of duress or undue influence, which indicates will No. 2 was a void document *ab initio* (from the beginning) and never had any effect. If you do execute a new will, the safest way to ensure that the first will can have no effect in the future is by tearing up or destroying the original and all copies.

## Partial Invalidity of a Will

Courts will go to extreme measures to follow a decedent's intentions. If a portion of a will is determined invalid but the remaining portion of the will is acceptable, courts can strike out the invalid portion and enforce the remaining parts. If the invalid portion defeats the intent of the will, the courts will void the entire document. A codicil (amendment) that does not revoke prior codicils which is inconsistent with a prior codicil will be given effect as if it revoked the prior codicil.

## Simultaneous Death

Most states have enacted simultaneous-death statutes, which provide that if there is an accident, such as a plane crash, and it is impossible to know who died first, and if title to property depends upon the priority of death, property shall be distributed as if each had survived the other. This is followed unless there is a provision in a will, trust, insurance policy, or other documentation to the contrary.

To avoid situations where it is impossible to determine who died first and whose will should control the distribution of property, a contingency clause for survival is included. If the husband does not survive his wife by thirty days, then the wife's gift to her husband fails, and her property is distributed in accordance with her will. Most wills contain a clause that states a spouse must survive the decedent (other spouse) by thirty days in order to receive the property of the decedent.

## Capacity

In order for someone to enter into a binding contract, draft a will, act as executor on a will or as a principal or agent on a power of attorney, the law requires that a person be eighteen years of age and of sound mind. The level of mental ability necessary to enter contracts or execute a valid will differs. One needs less mental ability to dispose of his property than to enter into a contract.

The issue of mental capacity and incapacity is similar to the issue of what is art and what is pornography; since perfectly sane educated people disagree, a court will decide. However, the issue of capacity versus incapacity is far more difficult for a court. The issue is not if a person is currently capable, but if that person was capable at the time the document was signed. A person also cannot be under undue influence in making or signing his will. If an elderly person suddenly changes her will and leaves all of her money to a housekeeper, there is a possibility the person was being wrongfully coerced into signing a new will. The new will would be void *ab initio*. Someone's old age, hardness of hearing, physical incapacity, crankiness, meanness, etc., have no bearing on the validity of the documents signed. The question of capacity is a factual issue that must be decided in each case.

In order to execute a valid will, a person must have sufficient mind and memory to:

- Understand the business he is undertaking
- Know the natural objects of his affection
- Know the character and extent of his property
- Form a plan in his mind

A person can believe there are bears running through the house and yet have the capacity to execute a valid will, provided the delusion does not affect the requirements listed in the above paragraph. By itself, a person's sickness (or inability to sign his name) is not reason enough to question his capacity to execute a will. The burden of proving lack of capacity rests with the party alleging the incapacity.

If you are in doubt about a person's capacity and believe a document may be subject to challenge, gather as much evidence (facts) as possible:

- Have a doctor provide a written opinion about that person's mental capabilities (at or near the time the person signs the document)
- Have documents notarized (which will provide an independent witness to the person's capacity)
- Have the person write a letter in his own handwriting describing his children and property (if possible)
- Keep social worker's interview notes (if possible)

## Executor's Duties

The executor is charged with the administration of the estate. Although he or she may hire attorneys to assist in the process, the executor has the ultimate responsibility to ensure that property is gathered, claims and taxes paid, and the will is followed. Some of the executor's duties include the following:

- The executor must preserve the estate even prior to issuance of *letters of office* from the court. The executor should take steps to ensure the property is protected from loss or waste.
- Follow funeral and burial instructions.
- Read the will and follow instructions in the will.
- Collect all property of the decedent.
- Pursue all possible claims the estate may be entitled to.
- Pay legitimate claims, debts, and taxes of the estate.
- File federal and state estate-tax returns.
- Keep an accounting and detailed records to enable the IRS to conduct an examination if it deems necessary.
- Pay spousal and minor's awards where applicable.
- Provide an accounting to the court if the estate is probated.
- Distribute property to beneficiaries and obtain receipts.

A checklist that follows can provide you and your lawyer with some items to consider when drafting a will or reviewing your current will. If the list contains items you are not clear about, ask your lawyer for a full explanation.

## Checklist for Wills

_____ Where is the location of the original will and any codicils?

_____ Does the will revoke all prior wills and codicils and reflect testator's current intentions?

_____ Has there been any significant personal or financial changes for either the testator or a beneficiary since the will was executed?

_____ Is there any writing or crossing out on the original will? If yes, draft a new will.

_____ Is the language in the will clear to the reader? Avoid ambiguous words.

_____ Make sure property specifically given to a beneficiary is still owned by the testator.

_____ If a specified number of shares of stock are gifted, have there been any stock splits or reverse splits that could change the amount of the intended gift?

_____ If real estate is gifted, include the exact legal description rather then a street address if possible.

_____ Where are copies of the trust agreements if they are listed in the will?

_____ Was the will witnessed and signed by at least two competent indi viduals above the age of eighteen who are not spouses, beneficiaries, or creditors? A witness cannot be considered unbiased and competent if he has an interest in the property.

_____ Does the will give property to individuals personally and not as married couples? This avoids future ambiguities caused by divorces, remarriages, and deaths of beneficiaries.

_____ Are there any individuals currently dependent on the testator for support, such as a spouse or disabled person? If yes, are they provided for under the will or a separate trust?

_____ Is the executor able to assume the duties of the office? Has a successor executor been named? Do you know the executor's current address and phone number?

_____ Does the will contain a _residuary clause?_

_____ Is the language in the will clear and concise with regard to specific gifts? Is the will specific as to what happens if an individual or a group member dies before the testator, while the will makes specific gifts to that individual or group of individuals?

_____ Does the will provide for a specific dollar amount of compensation for the executor? Although not required, paying at least a token amount is fair and equitable.

_____ If there have been advances or loans to any beneficiary, have these been accounted for in the will? Are the loans to be repaid or considered an addition to the inheritance?

_____ Does the will and titles to property take advantage of the unified credit if the estate has property in excess of $675,000 (2000 amount)?

_____ Has the testator considered allocating the GST exemption in his estate plans if he is leaving property to grandchildren?

_____ Does the will name a guardian for minor children and dependents?

_____ Has the testator considered including a deferred distribution trust in his will if he has minor children? This method defers distribution of their inheritance. For example, distribution could be ⅓ at age twenty-one, ⅓ at age twenty-five, with the balance at age thirty.

_____ Has the testator considered a QTIP trust if this is a second marriage? This trust allows the testator to provide income to his spouse for her life, yet control the disposition of the property upon her death. Otherwise, it may go to her new husband and not the testator's children.

_____ Does the will name as a beneficiary someone who is receiving state or federal assistance, such as Medicaid? If yes, consider drafting a new will. The beneficiary may already have a supplemental security income trust (SSI trust). If this is the case, the SSI trust should be named the beneficiary directly.

_____ Does the will effectively transfer property as intended if the testator has real property located in a different state?

_____ Is the estate-tax apportionment language the same in the will and trust agreements? Does one beneficiary end up paying all of the estate taxes from his share of the estate?

_____ If spouses have identical wills and plan on utilizing the unlimited marital deduction to defer estate taxes, are both spouses U.S. citizens? If not, consider a *qualified domestic trust (QDOT)*.

_____ If spouses have reciprocal wills and plan on utilizing the unlimited marital deduction to defer estate taxes, are there any encumbrances on the interest of property passing to the spouse? If yes, Internal Revenue Code §2056(b)(4)(B) may limit the amount of the unlimited marital deduction.

_____ If the testator has a business, has the executor been given the authority and power to continue and operate the business until a distribution can be made to the beneficiaries? If not, the executor only has the authority to preserve, not operate the business.

_____ Does the testator have a disabled beneficiary with a supplemental security income trust? If yes, make sure the trust is named the beneficiary, not the disabled individual directly.

_____ If the will makes a bequest to a charitable organization, consider obtaining a copy of the charity's §501(c)(3) determination letter from the IRS. You don't have to disclose the testator's name, and this will also ensure that you fill in the correct name of the charity.

_____ If this will is part of an overall estate plan with trusts, have you checked title to each piece of property, including ordering a title search on real estate to ensure the testator owns the property he is intending to bequeath?

_____ If you are the attorney who has drafted the will, have you forwarded a closing letter describing the scope of your representation to the client? For example, that it is the client's responsibility to fund trusts, contact brokers, and take care of other matters?

A sample will is included in the appendices for informational purposes. Consult with your own attorney when planning and drafting your will, since each state has its own specific requirements.

4

# Trusts

A trust is a legal fiction hundreds of years old where one person or company holds title to property for the benefit of another. All property has both a legal title and an equitable title. The trustee holds legal title and the beneficiary equitable title. There are numerous types and uses for trusts. Every trust has a *trustor* (person who puts property into a trust, also called a *grantor* or settlor), a trustee, trust property (Res), a trust agreement (instructions), and beneficiaries. There can be primary beneficiaries (those entitled to income currently) and remainder beneficiaries (those entitled to receive the principle after the primary beneficiaries have passed or a specific event has occurred). There also can be alternate beneficiaries who receive benefits if certain conditions occur. Trusts can be created during one's lifetime *(intervivos)* or at one's death (testamentary). Trusts can be drafted to allow changes at any time by the trustor (revocable or living trust) or drafted as permanent (irrevocable).

While most trusts and estates are separate taxable entities with their own rate schedules, some trusts, such as revocable living trusts, and *grantor trusts* are not taxed separately for federal-income-tax purposes, but have some or all of their income reported by the trustor or grantor.

## Points to Consider

• A trustee can bind a trust with his actions due to either his actual or apparent authority—so be careful when selecting a trustee.

- A living trust is considered a non-entity for income-tax purposes while the grantor is alive. You, as grantor, are not required to file tax returns for a living trust, since all of the income, capital gains, and expenses are reflected on your individual income-tax return.
- Fiduciary income-tax rates are higher than individual income-tax rates, so be careful when transferring income-producing property into an irrevocable trust. You must obtain a federal taxpayer identification number for an irrevocable trust, and file tax returns.
- Irrevocable trusts can be simple or complex for tax purposes. Each year, a simple trust must distribute all of its earnings, which are then taxed to the person receiving the distribution. A complex trust may accumulate or distribute earnings depending on the trust agreement. A trust may be simple one year and complex the next. When establishing a trust, check with your accountant to see if it is better to have a simple or complex trust.
- An election may be made under Internal Revenue Code §645 to treat revocable trusts as part of the estate. This may provide advantages in terms of tax deposits, passive activity losses, and charitable deductions.

## General Overview of Trusts

The majority of trusts are express trusts, which come into existence due to the legal intentions of the parties, as opposed to constructive trusts, which are created by operation of law. If a court finds that a person is holding property through fraud, or otherwise should not hold title to property, a court will impose a constructive trust, which will require the holder to care for and return the property to its lawful owner. A testamentary trust is generally funded by a will and springs into existence at the death of the trustor, but may be created and funded during one's lifetime. A living trust is one created and funded during your lifetime; it can be changed or canceled at any time by you. While living trusts are preferable to powers of attorney in managing the financial and personal affairs of an individual for a lengthy period of time, they can be an expensive option if one chooses a professional trustee, such as a bank.

Trusts can act like will substitutes and transfer property at death, thus circumventing probate proceedings, but there are matters in which a trust cannot perform, such as nominating guardians for minor children. A split-interest trust divides up the current and *future interests* in trust property and may have charitable and noncharitable beneficiaries. This may be described as "from A to B for life, remainder to C." Split interest means that there is a split between the current disposition of the trust and the future disposition. Certain split-interest trusts, such as a *charitable remainder annuity trust (CRAT)* and a *charitable remainder unitrust (CRUT)*, must have charitable and noncharitable beneficiaries.

Although trust agreements are generally private, there are times when the agreement, or a part thereof, must be disclosed, such as in the transfer of real property or in dealings with financial institutions.

Most irrevocable trusts cannot have related (family) persons act as trustees. See Internal Revenue Code §672(c). Irrevocable *charitable remainder trusts, grantor-retained income trusts (GRIT)*, and QTIP trusts, allow the grantor to act as the initial trustee.

Various types of trusts are created for individuals with special needs or for specific reasons. Recent federal laws significantly restrict previously used *Medicaid trusts*. Check the current laws in this area prior to drafting a trust agreement to avoid the Medicaid-prohibited transfers.

A trust must elect a calendar year end for reporting income while an estate may use a fiscal year. This means that an estate without a trust may elect tax-deferral techniques not available with trusts, unless an Internal Revenue Code §645 election is made to treat a trust as part of the estate. A representative may elect to include the income from a grantor trust, if the decedent held power over the trust, on the estate's fiduciary return for decedents dying after August 5, 1997. The election is made on the first return filed by the due date.

## Trust Agreements

Trust agreements should be in writing, signed by the trustor and trustee, and notarized. The agreement should contain the following:

- The agreement should state if the trustor retains the right to amend or revoke the trust agreement, and how amendments can be made.
- The agreement must contain the term of the trust, either specific in time or the life of an individual (watch for rule against perpetuities).
- The agreement should contain instructions regarding the disposition of trust income and corpus. You need to know if distributions are mandatory or discretionary, and when amounts are required to be distributed.

- The agreement should identify all powers granted to the trustee.
- The agreement usually provides that if a section is found to be invalid by a court of law, that section will be stricken with the remainder of the agreement remaining in full force and effect.
- The agreement should state which state's laws control interpretation of the agreement.
- The agreement must identify all beneficiaries and their future interests.

---

### TAX SAVINGS

A *qualified funeral trust (QFT)* may be established under §685 of the Internal Revenue Code. The election is made by filing Form 1041-QFT. The trustee reports income earned by the QFT, rather than the income being reported by the purchaser. The contribution limit to a QFT is $7,000 per beneficiary, provided the purpose of the trust is for funeral expenses and the trust has a contract with a professional funeral or burial service. See Internal Revenue Bulletin 1998-3, Notice 98-6, for additional information on a QFT.

---

## Abusive Trust Arrangements

The Internal Revenue Service issued a notice (Internal Revenue Bulletin No. 1997-16, April 21, 1997, Notice 97-24) that it intends to actively examine certain abusive trust arrangements that are sold by promoters. The promoters promise benefits under federal tax laws that do not exist. Examples of names used include the Business Trust, Equipment or Service Trust, Family Residence Trust, Charitable Trust, and Final Trust. The Internal Revenue Service generally follows substance over form in examining transactions for tax purposes. If you had planned to establish a charitable trust for current tax deductions with the charity being your son's or daughter's college education, plan again. The charity must be a legitimate organization, qualified for the tax deduction. If a salesman calls to describe the tax benefits of foreign trusts or one of the trusts listed above, check with your accountant or attorney prior to signing a contract. There are large penalties for abuse of the tax laws.

# Trustee's Duties

Trustees are subject to common law principles and state laws where trustee's duties have been enacted. In general, a trustee is charged with using the care, skill, prudence, and diligence of an ordinary person engaged in a similar business. A trustee is not expected to be perfect and will not be held responsible for errors in judgment if acting in good faith. If the trustee was selected because he professed to have greater expertise, he will be held to a higher standard. A trust agreement that contains a provision stating the trustee cannot be held accountable and relieves the executor from any responsibility will not be upheld by the courts. Trust provisions that reduce the standard of care to which the trustee is to be held are enforceable by the courts. The trustee must be fair to all beneficiaries, both life and remainder beneficiaries. Trustee's duties include, but are not limited to, the following list:

- Duty of good faith and loyalty to the trust. The trustee should not have any conflict of interests with the trust estate.
- Duty to follow the trust agreement. Deviations from the instructions can be found to be negligent, with damages assessed against the trustee.
- Duty to exercise reasonable care in dealings with all beneficiaries.
- Duty to collect and protect trust property from waste.
- Duty to exercise powers personally and not delegate responsibility.
- Duty to pay income to the beneficiaries.
- Duty to deal impartially with the trust, no self-dealing. A trustee should not profit from the trust.

# Estate-Planning Trusts

Several irrevocable trusts are used by estate planners to help people reduce the overall estate-tax burden. The key to remember is that estate taxes are assessed on property that you own or control at death. If you transfer property out of your control—for example, into irrevocable trusts—the property will not be included in your estate. Some of the trusts require that you outlive the term of the trust to enjoy the estate-tax advantages.

## IRREVOCABLE LIFE-INSURANCE TRUSTS

Life-insurance proceeds are included in a person's taxable estate if he or she had incidents of ownership or control of the policy at death. You can always give away the life-insurance policy to someone in order to take it out of your estate, but the person you give it to may not pay the premiums or may use the proceeds for their own benefit. You can establish an irrevocable life-insurance trust, and transfer ownership of the policy to the trust. You must do this at least three years prior to your death, or the proceeds will be included in your estate. You cannot be the trustee or retain any incidents of ownership on the policy. Once you have established the trust and transferred or purchased a policy, you can gift up to $10,000 per year per beneficiary to the trust in order to pay the premiums. In order for this to be a gift of a present interest that qualifies for the annual gift-tax exclusion, you must give the beneficiaries a reasonable amount of time to withdraw the money if they wish. This is called *Crummey powers.* If the beneficiaries do not withdraw the funds, the trustee uses these funds to pay the insurance premiums.

## QUALIFIED TERMINAL-INTEREST PROPERTY (QTIP) TRUSTS

One estate-planning method used by married couples involves QTIP trusts. In a QTIP trust, property is placed into a trust by the executor, and the QTIP election is made on the estate tax return. The property and all appreciation are then included in the second spouse's estate upon his or her death. Since the property may be tied up in an irrevocable trust for a number of years, only wealthier couples or couples involved in second marriages with children from a first marriage should consider a QTIP trust. The spouse has a life estate in the income from the QTIP property and must receive income at least annually. The surviving spouse, who is generally the trustee of the QTIP trust, may require that the trust sell assets to produce income. The advantage of the QTIP trust is that the first spouse designates the beneficiaries of the principal of the trust, rather than leaving all the property to her spouse outright. The trust agreement can provide that the surviving spouse is entitled to the principal for his education, health care, support, or maintenance. The agreement can also specify that the surviving spouse is entitled to the greater of 5 percent or $5,000 of the principal each year. The surviving spouse may be the trustee of the trust. This trust allows for significant postmortem planning, since although the trust must be drafted prior to death, it is the executor who elects to treat property as QTIP property and fund the trust. The executor can also make what is called a *reverse QTIP* election for generation-skipping transfer tax purposes for property placed into the trust. The reverse QTIP election will allow the executor to utilize the decedent's generation-skipping transfer tax exemption by treating the QTIP property as though it were passing directly from the decedent to the grandchildren rather than from the life beneficiary.

A QTIP may be designated as the beneficiary of an *individual retirement account (IRA)*. There are situations where an individual has remarried and wants the distributions from his IRA account to go to his spouse for life, but wants his children from his first marriage to receive the balance of the account upon his spouse's death. In order to qualify the IRA for QTIP treatment, you must take the following steps.

First, name the QTIP on the beneficiary-designation forms. Next, include in the QTIP agreement a provision giving the spouse the power to compel the IRA trustee to distribute all of the income earned by the IRA during the year. Finally, the executor should elect QTIP treatment for both the QTIP and the IRA. See Revenue Ruling 2000-2 for further explanation. A slight caution to consider when naming the QTIP the beneficiary of the IRA: If the spouse has the power to complete distribution of all the income from the trust but does not take the full distribution, the amount not taken may be considered a completed gift for gift-tax purposes, since the lapse of a power would be a reverse to the extent it exceeds $5,000 or 5 percent of the aggregate value of the assets per Internal Revenue Code §2514(e).

## QUALIFIED DOMESTIC TRUST (QDOT)
This trust must be used instead of the above QTIP trust if the spouse is not a citizen of the United States. See Revenue Procedure 96-54 for qualifying trust language.

## CREDIT SHELTER TRUST
This is an estate plan whereby the amount of property exempt from estate taxation by the decedent's unified credit is transferred to an irrevocable trust rather than directly to the spouse. This technique, also called an AB trust, bypasses the spouse's estate. The bypass trust designates a life beneficiary and final beneficiaries. Generally, the spouse is the life beneficiary. While the spouse cannot take ownership of the property, she may be given the right to invade the principal of the trust limited to $5,000 or 5 percent of the property, whichever is greater [Internal Revenue Code §2041(b)(2)]. The trustee may use the principal for the life beneficiary's health, education, support, and maintenance. If the spouse has a general power of appointment over the property, it will be included in her estate. Although the unlimited marital deduction shields property from federal

estate taxation when the first spouse dies, the decedent's unified credit cannot later be claimed by the surviving spouse when she dies. With proper planning and transferring titles to property so that each spouse has $675,000 (year 2000 exclusion amount) in property in his or her own name, a couple can shield $1.35 million in property transfers from estate taxation. Generally, the will or trust agreement directs the executor or trustee to place the unified-credit amount into a trust, with the remainder to the *marital deduction trust.*

## GRANTOR-RETAINED TRUST

Most grantor trusts have minimal advantages in estate planning, since the grantor generally retains control over the property transferred, and the property would be included in her estate. This is why living trusts do not save on estate taxes. When the grantor retains control over property, the gross income and capital gains and losses are reflected on grantor's individual income-tax return. Internal Revenue Code §§673–677 define the circumstances when income of the trust is taxed to the grantor for income-tax purposes. Treasury Regulation 1.671-1(a) provides income and deductions are reported by the grantor

- If the grantor has retained a reversionary interest in the trust within specified time limits
- If the grantor or a nonadverse party has certain powers over the beneficial interests
- If certain administrative powers over the trust exist under which the grantor can or does benefit
- If the grantor or a nonadverse party has a power to revoke the trust or return the corpus to the grantor
- If the grantor or a nonadverse party has the power to distribute income to or for the benefit of the grantor or the grantor's spouse

The above sections do not apply if the income of the trust is taxable to the spouse as maintenance or alimony. If the grantor contributed only a portion of the trust corpus, he will be taxed on his pro rata share. An adverse party is defined as any person holding a significant interest in the trust, which would be adversely affected by the exercise or nonexercise of a power that he possesses respecting the trust. A trustee is not an adverse party merely because he is acting as a trustee.

There are several irrevocable grantor trusts, which do provide estate-tax savings. These trusts are excellent techniques when the grantor or spouse has sufficient wealth and does not need the property. A grantor places property into a trust for a term of years and retains the income generated or use of the property with designated beneficiaries receiving the property at the end of the trust term. The grantor can be the trustee. Although the gift-tax exclusion is not available, since this is not a present gift but a future gift at the end of the term, the value of the gift for estate-tax purposes is its present value at the date of the transfer, reduced by the income stream to the grantor. For this technique to work to its full potential, the grantor must outlive the term of years of the agreement; otherwise, the remaining value of the trust (with appreciation) will be included in grantor's estate. One drawback to the grantor-retained trusts is that if the trust is funded with stocks and appreciating property, the ultimate beneficiaries will have to pay capital-gains taxes when they sell the property. If the grantor had kept ownership of the property, it would have received a step up in basis at death. There is no stepped-up basis for the trust property at the end of the trust.

There are several different types of grantor-retained trusts:

## GRANTOR-RETAINED ANNUITY TRUST (GRAT)

A grantor places property (excluding a personal residence) into a trust, with the trust paying the grantor a fixed amount annually for a specified number of years. At the end of the term, the property is transferred to the beneficiaries. The gift is valued at its worth at the time the property was placed into the trust, reduced by the annual payments. This technique can be used with the transfer of Subchapter S stock to family members at a discounted value. See IRS PLR 9444033. Since a GRAT is an irrevocable trust that must file a tax return each year, you can achieve additional tax savings by including language in the trust agreement that provides trust income and capital gains will be taxed to the grantor. The longer the term of the GRAT, the less the amount of gift tax that will be paid, since the grantor will be receiving payments for a number of years. The grantor must outlive the term of the GRAT, however, to receive the benefits.

## GRANTOR-RETAINED INCOME TRUST (GRIT)

This technique was popular until Congress passed the Revenue Reconciliation Act of 1990. A GRIT is similar to the above, but the trustee pays the income earned to the grantor each year. If the ultimate beneficiaries are family members, the tax savings are lost, and the grantor pays gift taxes on the full amount transferred into the trust. This is one of the few estate-tax savings devices single people may utilize—of course, they cannot take advantage of the unlimited marital deduction or a QTIP trust. Since a GRIT may be funded with a personal residence, this technique is often used to transfer vacation homes. In the case of a married couple, the grantor often includes in the trust agreement a statement that if the grantor's spouse dies, the house reverts back to the grantor. This defers estate taxes by allowing the couple to take advantage of the unlimited marital deduction. See Internal Revenue Code §2702 and Treasury Regulation 25.2702-5.

## GRANTOR-RETAINED UNITRUST (GRUT)
Similar to the GRAT, but the trust pays a fixed percentage of the net assets of the trust each year to the grantor. The trust must be appraised each year. One advantage is that the annual payments may increase to the grantor. The amount of gift tax to the beneficiary is calculated when the trust is established. A disadvantage to both a GRAT and a GRUT is that there can be only one funding of the principal. You cannot continue to add property to the GRAT or GRUT.

## QUALIFIED PERSONAL-RESIDENCE TRUSTS
Treasury Regulation §25.2702-5 allows individuals to establish qualified personal-residence trusts (QPRT). In general, a grantor transfers his interest in his principal residence or vacation home to a QPRT and retains both an interest and right to use the residence for a term of years. At the end of the term of years, the property passes to the QPRT beneficiaries (usually his children). This technique reduces the amount of estate tax, since: (1) the fair market value of the gift is calculated when transferred into the trust, and has a reduced value due to the grantor's retained interest; and (2) any appreciation in value of the property is excluded from grantor's estate. If the grantor dies before the term of years, the entire property is included in his estate but an adjustment is made for taxable gifts so the property is not taxed twice. Basically, if the grantor dies before the end of the term, the estate taxes are the same as though the QPRT never existed.

In order for the trust agreement to qualify as a QPRT, the instrument must contain specific provisions, which are beyond the scope of this book. In order to establish a QPRT and take advantage of this excellent estate-planning technique, contact an attorney familiar with QPRT's.

## LAND TRUST

A land trust is a means of holding title to real property, which is allowed by several states. Illinois allows an Illinois trustee to hold title to real property located in the state. A bank will act as trustee and charge a nominal fee for setting up the land trust and an annual fee for acting as trustee. The land trust will have no effect on your Illinois *homestead exemption.* This is a method of avoiding probate for the residence, but it does not save on estate taxes.

## ADVANTAGES OF A LAND TRUST

**Avoids Probate**
Property is transferred by the trustee to the beneficiaries as provided for in the agreement.

**Private**
The identity of beneficiaries is not a matter of public record.

**Avoids Partition**
The beneficiaries cannot file a suit for partition of the property.

**One trustee for multiple owners**
If there are multiple owners, it may be easier to have one party—the trustee—sign all of the mortgage and other documents. It also facilitates changes in beneficial ownership interests.

**Personal Liability**
It only the trustee signs the notes, the beneficiaries will not be personally liable in a foreclosure suit.

## DISADVANTAGES OF A LAND TRUST

**Initial Cost**
The bank will charge a fee to establish and place property in trust.

**Annual Fee**
Annual fee to the trustee.

**Limitations**
An Illinois land trustee has no duties to manage or preserve the property, whereas the trustee of a living trust has a fiduciary obligation to preserve the property.

*(continued)*

*(continued from previous page)*

### Medicaid

As discussed previously, if a person wishes to avoid the *spend-down* rules to be eligible for Medicaid assistance, property placed into a trust is subject to a five-year look-back period rather than three years. Placing your real property into an Illinois land trust may cause a longer look-back period.

### Beneficial Interests

The beneficiary's interest in a land trust is considered personal property. In some states, personal property is treated differently from real property for bankruptcy, divorce, and estate-tax matters. If you place your real property into a land trust and then move to another state, check with an attorney in your new state to determine the effect the land trust will have on your plans.

# Checklist for Trusts

_____ Do you have a copy of each trust instrument and amendment?

_____ Is the trust agreement signed and notarized?

_____ Has all the property been placed into the trust (is the trust funded)? Is there an attachment describing the trust property?

_____ Do you know the phone number and address of the trustee?

_____ Does the trust agreement properly reflect the trustor's current intentions?

_____ Does the trust agreement reflect any advances or loans to beneficiaries?

_____ Are there any specific trusts described in the will that you do not have copies of?

_____ Do you have copies of trust tax returns filed (Form 1041) for the last five years if the trust is an irrevocable trust?

_____ Is the trustee aware of his duties and responsibilities?

_____ Does the trust allow an agent (power of attorney) to make gifts of trust property?

_____ Does the trust instrument clearly identify the beneficiaries, specify the purposes of the trust, how the trust is to be performed, and how it can be amended?

_____ If this is an irrevocable life-insurance trust, has the trustee been sending letters to the beneficiaries each year advising them of their right to withdraw the gift within a reasonable time (*Crummey* powers)? If not, there could be gift-tax problems.

_____ Is the estate-tax apportionment language the same in the trust agreements and will? Does one beneficiary end up paying all of the estate taxes from his share of the estate?

_____ If this is a credit-shelter trust, does the spouse possess a general power of appointment over trust property? If she has the power, the purpose of the trust will be lost. Does the trust agreement clearly indicate that the spouse may not use trust property to satisfy her legal obligations? If the spouse has unlimited access to the property, it will be included in her estate.

_____ If this is a qualified terminal-interest property trust, does the agreement clearly state that the spouse is entitled to trust income at least annually?

_____ If you are a successor trustee, has there been any accountings over trust property? Have there been previous distributions to beneficiaries?

_____ If the trustor intends to make gifts to the trust, which qualify for the annual gift-tax exclusion, have annual notices been sent to the beneficiaries notifying them of their right to withdraw the funds? If not, the gifts may not qualify for the *annual exclusion*.

——— Has there been any writing or crossing out on the original trust agreement that may invalidate part or all of the agreement? If yes, draft a new trust agreement.

——— If this is a marital-deduction trust, does the estate plan call for estate administration expenses to be paid out of the trust assets? If yes, the benefits of the unlimited marital deduction will be lost for those expenses. See §2056(b)(4)(B) of the Internal Revenue Code.

——— If this is a marital-deduction trust, did the testator direct his spouse to pay any legacies or otherwise direct the funds? If yes, the benefits of the unlimited marital deduction will be lost for the amount of the legacies or other payments.

——— If the surviving spouse is the trustee of the QTIP trust, does she have a good relationship with the ultimate beneficiaries? If not, consider a cotrustee to manage the QTIP trust to avoid conflicts.

——— If this is a qualified personal-residence trust, review the following:

- Does the grantor already have an interest in more than two QPRT's? If yes, this QPRT will not qualify.
- Does the property in the QPRT consist of property other than a residence or vacation home the grantor has the right to use at all times, and a sufficient amount of cash to meet expenses?

——— Does the trust agreement specifically authorize the trustee to disclaim property or disclaim the power to invade corpus on behalf of a beneficiary when allowed by state law? If state law allows a *disclaimer,* the trust agreement should give this power to the trustee. Even if state law allows it, the authority must be given to the trustee in the trust agreement, or he cannot utilize it. If allowed by state law and provided for in the trust agreement, this may assist in postmortem tax planning.

——— If the testator has a QTIP trust, consider placing express language in the agreement, allowing the trustee to allocate the trust into two trusts, one of which uses up the remainder of the testator's GST exemption, the other for non-GST exemption property. See §2652(a)(3) of the Internal Revenue Code.

_____ If this is a charitable remainder trust, have you complied with state registration requirements?

_____ If you are transferring property into an irrevocable trust, have you filed a Form 709 (Gift-Tax Return) or Form 8283 (Noncash Charitable Contributions), and secured appraisals of the property?

# 5

# Living Trusts

A living trust is an estate-planning technique that one uses during his lifetime to control property placed into a trust while he is able to manage his affairs. If and when he is unable to manage his affairs, a trustee he has already selected handles his affairs. It is an intervivos (during lifetime) revocable (can be changed or amended at any time) trust. One should be careful in deciding on using a living trust. Many promoters (who must be qualified to practice law if they are drafting legal documents) want to sell you a living trust so you can avoid probate and, allegedly, save thousands of dollars in attorney fees. This may or may not turn out to be true. You may end up paying more to set up and transfer assets into the trust than the probate costs would be without the trust. You also may end up going through probate for some other reason even if you have the trust. A living trust may also cost you thousands of dollars in lost Medicaid benefits due to the extended prohibited transfer rules for trusts. There are other advantages to living trusts, however. They can provide long-term care for an individual and they are contested far less frequently than wills.

If you have drafted a durable power of attorney for property and granted someone the authority over your financial affairs in case you are unable to act, add specific language in the power of attorney granting that person the power to add property to your living trust. The trustee has only the power over property in the trust.

## Points to Consider

- A living trust does not save on federal estate taxes, since the property is under the control of the trustor, but it will save on probate costs, since property in the trust passes outside of probate.
- It is rare that a beneficiary will contest a living trust. Will contests happen frequently and cost time and money.
- A living trust is the preferable vehicle for the long-term care of individuals. The trustor is able to leave detailed instructions in the agreement regarding how he wants his property managed and distributed.
- In order to achieve the full benefits of a living trust, the trustor must continue to place new property into the trust.
- A living trust and a living will are two completely separate documents with no relation to one another. A living will is a health-care directive, while a living trust is a form of property ownership or contract.
- Living trusts are often combined with credit shelter (AB), marital, qualified terminal-interest property (QTIP), and other trusts in the same document.

## General Overview of Living Trusts

The living trust is an ancient concept from English common law. In its early stages, the living trust was used by the English nobility to transfer their landholdings without undue interference from the government. Living trusts are now valid in all states. This estate-planning technique, once used only by the wealthy, is now preferred by a lot of ordinary citizens. Living trusts are frequently mentioned in the media and by promoters holding seminars. A living trust is an intervivos trust created by the trustor for the benefit of a beneficiary (himself). A living trust can be revoked or amended at any time prior to the death or incapacity of the trustor, allowing changes to the estate plans. Property held in a living trust does not go through probate, but goes to the named beneficiaries upon the death of the trustor. Since the trustee has a fiduciary duty to preserve and protect the trust assets, and because of the detailed instructions the trustor can include in the agreement, the living trust is the preferred technique for the long-term care of individuals. Living trusts are often referred to as will substitutes, although everyone should also have a will. Individuals with living trusts generally have a "pour-over" will. After making any specific bequests and paying claims, the will provides that all property be placed in the living trust.

Living trusts are contested less frequently than wills. The legal capacity necessary to make a valid will is low. One needs only to know the natural objects of his affection. Wills are often contested based on undue influence, duress, menace, or fraud. Since a trustor will meet with attorneys and discuss the living-trust agreement and generally act as the initial trustee, it is hard to believe that the trustor failed to have the capacity to execute a valid trust or was under undue influence.

Any number of trusts can be created in one single document. Generally, the initial trustee is the trustor. There are named successor-trustees, to step in upon the incapacity of the trustor. The trustor can name cotrustees if he wishes, although if they disagree, this could lead to problems. Husbands and wives can execute a joint living-trust agreement. The trust agreement should contain detailed instructions to the trustee. A living trust has another benefit over a will. It can be used for the care of its maker while incapacitated, but a will has no effect until a person dies.

## Transferring Property to a Living Trust

It may be that certain property should not be transferred into a living trust. Placing real and personal property into the trust is referred to as "funding" the trust. Prior to transferring all of your property into the trust, check with your attorney and accountant. If you have an IRA account and you wish to make your trust the beneficiary of the account, the age of the trust beneficiaries may affect the tax deferral time for the IRA. For example, if you make the trust the beneficiary of the IRA account, and the beneficiaries of your trust are older than your other heirs, the trust beneficiaries may have to start paying taxes on the money sooner than a younger heir would, because they are at the age where they are required to make withdrawals from the IRA.

If you are placing real property (residence) into a trust, check with the mortgage holder first to make sure placing the property into a trust does not trigger an acceleration clause in the mortgage (the bank may tell you to pay the entire balance at once).

If you own closely held stock, there may be restrictions on transferring legal ownership. Check with the stock-transfer agent. Generally, Subchapter S stock cannot be transferred into a living trust except for a very short period of time. In some states, placing real property into a trust changes the character of the property to personal property with possible loss in creditor-protection rights.

The IRS has ruled that the exclusion of gain on the sale of a principal residence is allowed even though the residence is in a living trust.

## ADVANTAGES OF A LIVING TRUST

### Fiduciary
A living trust is the preferable vehicle for long-term financial management and care for a disabled person's affairs. The trustee of a living trust has a duty to act, whereas an attorney-in-fact, acting as agent, does not have a duty to act. The agent on a power of attorney can resign, whereas a trustee has a duty to continue in office until replaced.

### Privacy
Trusts are more private than a will, and do not have to be filed with the clerk's office. However, there are situations where the trust will have to be disclosed.

### Lawsuits
Transfers to the beneficiaries at death are contested less frequently than transfers under wills.

### Avoids Probate
A living trust will help avoid probate.

### Asset Protection
A living trust may help shield property from creditors.

### Inheritance
A living trust may prevent the spousal claim for inheritance (statutory right to marital property), provided there is no intent to defraud.

## DISADVANTAGES OF A LIVING TRUST

### Costs
There are higher initial and annual expenses than with a will. Everyone with a living trust should also have a will. In addition, a poorly drafted trust may be open to multiple interpretations, which could lead to far more complications and expense than if it had never existed.

### Gifting
In general, a trust cannot make gifts. If your property is in trust, transfer property from the trust to yourself, and then to the person to whom you are making a gift.

*(continued)*

*(continued from previous page)*

### Medicaid
Property transferred into a trust is subject to a sixty-month (five-year) Medicaid disallowance (spend-down) rule rather than thirty-six months. Also, the trustee may have a fiduciary duty to pay for your health-care costs rather than allowing Medicaid to pay the costs.

### Probate
Creditor cutoff period for claims is generally two years with a living trust rather than six months with probate proceedings. If the living trust goes through probate, as when a testator executes a will that pours over into the living trust, it then has the same claims time frame as regular probate. If you execute a living trust but fail to fund it, your estate may end up going through probate anyway. If the decedent had a potential lawsuit at his death, his estate will be opened up regardless of the living trust.

### Property
Check your state laws to make certain that placing your residence in a living trust will not affect any homestead exemption. If you name your living trust the beneficiary of your IRA account, you may decrease the tax-deferral period if there is an older person who is named a beneficiary in your Living Trust.

### Subchapter S Stock
Except for a certain type of trust, a trust cannot own Subchapter S stock for more than sixty days.

### Tax payments
If the living trust were to become an irrevocable trust (such as by the death of the grantor), it would be required to make quarterly estimated tax payments if the property was not distributed immediately rather than the two-year grace period allowed for estates and grantor trusts, unless Internal Revenue Code §645 election is made. Section 645, *Certain Revocable Trusts Treated as Part of Estate,* allows the estate executor and trustee of a qualified revocable trust to treat and tax the trust as part of the estate.

A sample living trust is included in the appendices for your review. Since each person's situation is different and the laws vary from state to state, consult with your attorney when drafting a living trust. The following checklist covers many of the issues that you may wish to consider and discuss with your attorney when planning your living trust.

## Checklist for Living Trusts

_____ Does trustor have the power to modify the agreement?

_____ Does trustor have the power to terminate the trust?

_____ Can the trustor add additional property to the trust from any source including wills, and take property from the trust?

_____ Discuss how to determine if the trustor is incapacitated. Should his primary physician alone be the person to make the determination?

_____ How should expenses and claims incurred upon the trustor's death be handled? Should taxes and claims be paid by the executor or trustee?

_____ Discuss the distribution of property to the beneficiaries and what happens if a beneficiary predeceases the trustor. Should the property go to the beneficiary's descendants or revert to the trust?

_____ Consider a section whereby you, as trustor, include all of your children to include adopted children, and any child born after your death.

_____ Name the initial trustees and successor trustees. Do you want cotrustees?

_____ Name any specific gifts you would like to make before distributions.

_____ Name all the beneficiaries.

_____ Consider distributions to minors. Should minor's shares vest immediately but minor to receive the income distributions on a quarterly basis? Do you wish to consider a deferred distribution trust where minors receive a percent of the principal at different ages?

_____ What if a beneficiary is under a legal disability? Should there exist a separate trust for his benefit?

_____ Include a section that states distributions are not subject to attachment by creditors.

_____ Grant the power to the trustee to terminate any trust in existence with a balance less than a certain dollar amount, perhaps $25,000.

_____ Discuss the powers that you wish to grant your trustee:

- The right to commingle trust assets
- The right to sell or lease real and personal property
- The right to enter into investments
- The right to buy and sell stocks and bonds, and to participate in voting shares of stocks
- The right to borrow money if necessary in the administration of the trust
- The right to employ attorneys, accountants, and agents
- The right to determine what is income or principal
- The right to make *generation-skipping tax* elections if the trustor has not done so
- The right to manage business interests
- The right to conduct any additional acts necessary to manage the trusts

_____ Discuss how trustees are appointed and how they can be removed, possibly by a majority of the beneficiaries.

_____ Generally, you wish to make the trustee not liable for any losses, provided she uses reasonable care and due diligence in managing the trust.

_____ If you are naming a charitable organization, make sure you have the correct legal name.

_____ Review the property that you wish to place in the living trust. Make sure there are no adverse consequences of placing the property into the trust.

_____ Should the agreement contain a credit-shelter trust, a QTIP trust, and a marital trust so the trustee can take maximum advantage of estate-planning opportunities?

_____ Does the trustor have a "pour-over" will? Generally, if the trustor is using a living trust to avoid probate, it doesn't seem to make sense having a "pour-over" will that will have to go through probate. However, this allows all property not placed into the living trust during the trustor's life to be placed into the living trust for estate-administration purposes.

_____ Have the trust agreement notarized so that the trustee will be able to sell real estate.

_____ Make sure the trustor signs the agreement as trustor and initial trustee.

# 6

# Power of Attorney

A power of attorney is a legal document whereby you grant another party the right to act on your behalf to do something you could have done. The person to whom you grant this power does not have to be an attorney or relative. There are many times when you need someone to act on your behalf. If you are selling your home, you may grant your attorney the power to sign loan documents or deeds. If you are planning an extended European vacation and want your daughter to run the family business, you may want to give her the authority to manage the business.

A power of attorney is a grant of authority by one person to another. This chapter discusses various powers of attorney. General powers of attorney are generally limited to simple transactions. Durable powers of attorney generally allow the agent to perform all acts that the principal could perform, and remain in force even if the principal becomes incapacitated. Springing powers of attorney will "spring" into effect at a certain time in the future, or when a specific event occurs.

## Points to Consider

- A power of attorney cannot be used to designate a person to act as guardian for your children; you can only nominate a person with a will.
- A power of attorney cannot be used to designate a person as a property guardian for your children's property if you die; again, you need to nominate the person with a will. However, you can use a

durable power of attorney to manage your children's property if you become incapacitated. Remember, even a durable power of attorney becomes invalid when the principal dies.

- Powers of attorney are dangerous legal documents. The principal, creator of the document, is granting an agent almost unlimited authority over their property without supervision.

- The agent, unlike a trustee, does not have a duty to act and may resign at any time. Successor agents should always be named on powers of attorney.

- A person can create springing powers of attorney, which take effect at some future date or event, such as when the principal is determined by his personal physician to be incapable of managing his financial affairs.

## General Powers of Attorney

Within the common law principles of agency and contracts, an individual is able to grant another person or company authority to act on his behalf. The principal and agent must both be at least eighteen years of age and of sound mind. The authority of the agent is limited to the authority of the principal. If the principal becomes incapacitated and unable to enter a contract, the agent is also considered incapacitated and unable to enter contracts. General powers of attorney are usually limited to one particular transaction, such as to sell my house on June 25, but can be unlimited in scope and duration.

A general power of attorney terminates on the death of the principal, when he becomes incapacitated, or the specific grant of authority is complete.

If an agent on a power of attorney fraudulently transfers the principal's property to himself, courts will recover the property, if it still exists. When a person is acting in a fiduciary relationship as a matter of law, such as attorney-client, accountant-client, or as a matter of fact, such as principal-agent, courts will look for a breach of the fiduciary relationship and return the property. For the issue of undue influence courts look for the following factors, which must be proven by clear and convincing evidence:

- Fiduciary relationship
- Decedent trusted the agent
- Beneficiary caused the document to be prepared
- Beneficiary received substantial benefits

EXAMPLE    A woman placed her grandmother's assets in a joint account with her with rights of survivorship. The court found the presumption of fraud outweighed the presumption of donative intent.

Some of the issues to be considered when drafting powers of attorney include the following:

- Should the agent receive compensation?
- At what date should the power take effect; should it spring into action at some future date or event?
- How should the principal's incapacity be determined?
- Does the agent need to keep records?
- Are there restrictions on self-dealing by the agent?
- What authority exactly does the agent have? Can the agent name guardians or change the terms of a trust?
- Who should be the successor agent?

## Durable Powers of Attorney for Property

States recognize the inherent limitations on general powers of attorney. All states have enacted some form of the durable power of attorney in their statutes (all durable powers of attorney should follow the language of their state of origin, word for word). A power of attorney is needed most when a person becomes incapacitated, but general powers at that time have no effect. These durable powers of attorney continue in full force and effect during the principal's incapacitated period until death. They are very powerful legal documents. The agent has almost unlimited power over the principal's property with very little supervision. The document can be revoked by being torn up. While the document does not have to be recorded after execution, if it is used to transfer real estate, it will be recorded in the county recorder's office.

Recent changes to some state's laws provide protection for persons relying on an apparently valid power of attorney. This amendment solves a problem for banks and financial institutions that rely on apparently valid powers of attorney, which turn out to be forged documents.

The Internal Revenue Service has held that gifts made by an agent with a durable power of attorney are not valid gifts for federal estate- and gift-tax purposes unless the durable power of attorney includes express language that the agent has the power to make such gifts (see IRS PLR 9410028). The result of this ruling is that if the express language is not included in the document, the gifts are included in the gross estate of the decedent, and additional estate taxes might have to be paid. If you encounter this situation, check your state law requirements concerning capacity of a *donor* to make gifts. The federal law concerning gifts looks to the state law regarding capacity.

## Checklist for Durable Powers of Attorney for Property

_____ Has the principal read and understood the entire document?

_____ Is there any writing or crossing out on the original copy, which may invalidate the document? If yes, draft a new power of attorney.

_____ Is the power of attorney signed, dated, and notarized?

_____ Is the agent the correct person to make decisions?

_____ Is the agent competent and at least eighteen years of age?

_____ Is a successor agent named?

_____ Are the effective dates on the power valid?

_____ Does the power of attorney grant all powers needed, such as the power to make gifts, add property to a living trust, or create additional powers of attorney?

_____ Does a trust agreement allow a power of attorney to be used if gifting property from the trust, and does the power of attorney specifically mention gifting from this trust?

A sample durable power of attorney is included in the appendices for your review. Again, make sure you use your state's language when drafting a durable power of attorney.

# Health-Care Power of Attorney

The statutory health-care power of attorney is a medical directive that provides instructions on the final care to be given a person, and related issues. This document differs from a living will in that it designates an agent to make decisions for a specific time frame, although it can be indefinite. At the moment a medical directive is needed most, the agent named may be unable to act in accordance with the person's intentions (perhaps a son or daughter cannot tell the doctor to withhold further life-sustaining measures). A living will is directed at the health-care provider without an agent. The living will directs the doctor not to use extraordinary life-sustaining measures, but does not contain the other provisions contained in the health-care power of attorney.

The health-care power of attorney does not have to be notarized or recorded to be valid. In general, only one witness's signature is needed. The document can be revoked by being torn up. The health-care power of attorney contains provisions for items other than withholding life-sustaining treatment. There are sections (which can be deleted by the principal) allowing the agent to make decisions concerning autopsies, organ donations, and other issues.

The health-care power-of-attorney laws provide that death resulting from the withholding of life-sustaining treatment is not to be considered suicide, and does not affect provisions in any life-insurance policies.

In general, a power of attorney for health care supersedes a living will executed by a person, as long as the agent is available.

A sample health-care power of attorney is included in the appendices for your review.

# Checklist for Health-Care Power of Attorney

_____ Has the principal read and understood the entire document?

_____ Is the agent competent and at least eighteen years of age?

_____ Is the document signed and witnessed?

_____ Is there any writing or crossing out on the original copy, which may invalidate the document? If yes, draft a new health-care power of attorney.

_____ Is the agent the correct person to make decisions?

_____ Does the agent know he or she is named as agent on the document?

_____ Has the principal considered executing a living will in addition to the health-care power of attorney?

# Information for Executors and Administrators

I f you are appointed as an executor or administrator of an estate, you
will want to read this chapter, which includes steps and checklists to
follow in handling the estate. This chapter also contains checklists for
the professionals who will be helping you to manage the estate. You can
use these to help you understand exactly what the responsibilities of these
professionals are, and also to follow up and ascertain that all is proceeding
as it should.

You should not try to close the estate without guidance. Find an
attorney who can prepare the necessary documents and guide you through
the process. The executor checklist should be helpful in providing
reminders of steps needed to close the estate. Remember that an executor
or administrator may be held personally liable if he does not proceed with
due diligence in handling the estate, and liable for federal estate taxes if
distributions are made without taxes being paid.

## Points to Consider

- If you are named the executor or executrix in a will, you are responsible for preserving the estate of the decedent even prior to a court
  issuing you letters of office. Take action immediately if property
  may be lost.
- When hiring an attorney, obtain a written contract and determine
  in advance if the attorney will charge by the hour or a percentage of
  the gross estate.

- The estate will remain open a minimum of six and one half months, which will allow time for creditors to file claims and allow those who may wish to contest the will to file petitions (such as claiming the will was created under undue influence or duress). Only parties interested in a decedent's property, such as beneficiaries, may contest the validity of a will.
- For federal estate-tax filing requirements, if there is no appointed executor, personal representative, or administrator of the decedent's estate, then any person in actual or constructive possession of the decedent's property is considered an executor and must file the estate-tax return.

# Probate

In general, probate is the process of transferring title to a decedent's property. Probate also establishes guardians and *conservators* for minors and adults with legal disabilities. The courts that handle probate proceedings have different names in each state. The process does not have to be the time-consuming, wealth-destroying administrative nightmare depicted in movies, books, and by living-trust promoters. In Illinois, there are simplified procedures, such as independent administration, that allow minimal court supervision. Independent administration allows the executor or administrator to handle the affairs of the estate—such as selling real estate and making distributions—without first obtaining court approval. With *supervised administration,* the attorney or executor is constantly going to court filing documents and seeking a judge's permission to perform some act for the estate.

The probate court handles property that is in the decedent's name alone. Many assets, such as insurance policies, annuities, individual retirement accounts, trust assets, and jointly owned property, pass outside of probate.

Probate must be conducted in each state the decedent owned real property *(ancillary probate)* unless the property is in a trust. In general, a small-estate affidavit may be used in lieu of probate if probate property is less than $50,000 (and not real estate). This affidavit may help to avoid having to go to court and can be used to transfer title to stocks, cars, boats, and other personal items.

Check with your local court clerk to see if there are brochures that will walk you through the probate process.

## Advantages to Going through Probate

- The probate court provides a judicial finding that a document is, in fact, a decedent's valid last will and can be relied upon by all parties.
- The probate court appoints an administrator for the estate if no valid will can be found.
- A notice of death is published in a newspaper, which will establish time frames (cutoff periods) for creditors and those who plan to contest the will.
- The probate court determines the validity of claims.
- Periodic accountings are filed with the court in supervised administration proceedings to protect the property and beneficiaries involved.
- The probate court will appoint guardians for minor children and their property.

## Disadvantages to Going through Probate

- Probate takes time and generally costs more than having a trustee of a living trust close the estate.
- Since most court documents are public information, there is a loss of privacy when going through probate.
- Absence of complete control over wrapping up affairs of the estate.

## Checklist for Executors

(The following is a list of steps an executor may follow in closing an estate. Additional steps may be needed for your estate, such as necessary to satisfy a specific state law requirement.)

I.     Preliminary Steps

_____   Take steps to secure valuable property if the decedent's residence will be vacant until sold (especially during the funeral, since this is an open notice to burglars that a home will be vacant). Turn off utilities not needed, such as telephone and cable.

_____   Search for original will and file with clerk of the court in the county in which the decedent resided as soon as possible; do not wait more than thirty days. You can receive a certified copy upon payment of a small fee; request at least five copies.

_____ Contact the funeral home and follow any funeral instructions the decedent made.

_____ Read the will and all codicils. It is the executor's responsibility to ensure that the will instructions are followed.

_____ Request at least thirty copies of the death certificate (generally from the funeral director). Original copies are needed to transfer stock, file with insurance companies, transfer property, and for other purposes.

_____ Open a bank account in the estate's name (for an estate account, a bank will ask for a letter of office from the court), which pays interest while you are going through probate, and use it for all receipts and disbursements of the estate. Do not commingle personal funds with the estate's funds.

_____ Open a bank account, which pays interest, in your own name if you are not going through probate. (Without letters of office, you may not be able to open an account in the name of the estate.) Deposit receipts and pay expenses from this account.

_____ Determine whether immediate steps are needed to preserve the value of a business if the decedent was operating as a sole owner. Discuss with attorney to ensure you have the authority to act on behalf of the company.

_____ Check the status of all real property that is in the decedent's name. Contact insurance companies to make sure sufficient insurance coverage is in effect, contact tenants and inform them how and where to pay rent. Do not take immediate possession of real estate occupied by an heir of the decedent as a personal residence unless the will provides otherwise.

II.     Administration of the Estate

_____ Sign a written contract with the attorney, if one is hired. The attorney will represent the executor. The agreement should state who will be responsible for which items and how attorney fees will be calculated.

_____ Inventory safe-deposit boxes and search for the original will and property. It is best to have a witness, such as the attorney, with you.

_____ If the estate is subject to probate, have the attorney get you copies of letters testamentary from the court.

_____ Keep copies of all receipts and expenses.

_____ File a change of address to obtain decedent's mail if necessary. This is especially important at the beginning of the year, when tax information documents are mailed. You will need the information for tax returns.

_____ Check that real estate taxes (if paid in installments by the decedent rather than a bank) are paid up to date.

_____ Contact payers of pension benefits and annuities, Social Security Administration, Railroad Retirement Board, employer, investment companies, and others, and notify them of decedent's death to allow them to stop benefits. Return checks for amounts paid for days after date of death. The decedent could be receiving payments through Electronic Fund Transfer direct to his accounts; be careful of spending money that is not the decedent's.

_____ Contact the Social Security Administration or the Railroad Retirement Board if there is a surviving spouse with minor children for benefit purposes.

_____ Contact the Social Security Administration for the (modest) burial benefit and the Veterans Administration for flag and any benefits that may be due, if the funeral director did not take care of contacting the agencies.

_____ Notify the decedent's employer of death. Check for unpaid wages, accrued vacation pay, and pension plans. Inquire regarding employee death benefits.

_____ Determine if the decedent was a party to any lawsuit or died with a possible cause of action (potential lawsuit). Inform the attorney of any possible litigation.

_____ Notify all clubs or fraternal organizations where the decedent was a member. Check if there are any death benefits, credit unions, insurance policies.

_____ Cancel all credit cards and subscriptions. If possible, pay off the balance when notifying the companies of the decedent's death to save additional charges.

_____ If you are the representative of an estate, you have a duty to contest an *IRS levy* if warranted, or you could be held personally responsible for the debt.

_____ Determine if there are any deficiencies on income-tax returns filed for the last three years or if any returns are being audited. Since the executor is responsible for ensuring that all debts are paid, do not distribute any of decedent's property until all taxes and debts are paid or reserved for in accounts.

_____ Notify insurance companies of decedent's death. If you do not know which policies were still in effect on the date of decedent's death, do the following: Check the decedent's address and telephone book for agent names.

_____ Check the decedent's checkbook for the last several years for insurance payments.

_____ Check the decedent's mail for a year after date of death searching for notices of premium payments due.

_____ Review income tax returns for the past several years for interest expenses paid to insurance companies and dividends or interest paid by insurance companies.

_____ Check with the state's unclaimed property office (in a couple of years) to see if a company has turned over proceeds to the state.

_____ Contact as many of the largest insurance companies as you can and provide them the decedent's name and social security number; they can generally check for current policies while you hold on the phone.

_____ Check if the decedent was custodian of any minor's accounts. If yes, notify the company so the subsequent custodian named will receive notices. If the minor is twenty-one years of age, request a distribution to him or her.

_____ If the decedent was the owner of insurance policies on her children, the children probably became the owners of the policies. Notify the companies and advise the children, if adults, that it will be their choice to continue paying the premiums or request the cash-surrender value.

_____ Make a complete list of the decedent's property and debts. Include contracts the decedent may have signed (such as a contract to build a house or purchase a car), which are not complete. Notify the other party to the contract and the attorney.

_____ Determine if the decedent was a partner in any partnership or trust and notify them of death. Inquire as to decedent's basis and forms needed to transfer ownership.

_____ If a decedent signs a contract to transfer property specifically bequeathed in his will, and the contract remains executory at time of death, this does not act like a revocation but instead the beneficiary receives the property subject to the contract.

_____ Obtain appraisals for all property with a combined value of $3,000 or more if a Form 706, United States Estate (and Generation-Skipping Transfer) Tax Return, must be filed. If a return is not required, appraisals may be helpful for any future IRS audit when the beneficiaries sell inherited property.

_____ If the estate includes real property located within twenty-five miles of a metropolitan area, national forest or wilderness area, or ten miles of an urban national forest, and all persons who have an interest in the property would agree to sign an agreement to prohibit surface mining or commercial development of the real property, consider making this election on the estate-tax return, consequently reducing the value of the estate. This is an irrevocable election.

_____ Contact stock-transfer agents to obtain forms necessary to transfer ownership of stocks and bonds. When mailing completed forms with stock certificates, send by registered mail, return receipt requested, and insure the certificates.

_____ Obtain receipts from beneficiaries when making distributions.

_____ Generally, you do not make distributions to an ex-spouse even if listed in the will. If the decedent divorced (or the marriage was declared invalid) after signing her will, the ex-spouse is treated as though deceased for all gifts, interests, and powers of appointment. Check with the attorney for your state's law on this issue.

_____ Obtain a written disclaimer prior to distributing any property to a beneficiary if the person does not want to inherit the property from the will (such as for estate-tax purposes). A later disclaimer may not be valid.

_____ Use small-estate affidavits to transfer title to personal property (cars, boats, stock, etc.) if the estate has probate property less than $50,000 and you have not applied for letters of office from the probate court.

_____ Make partial distributions to beneficiaries when you are certain funds are sufficient to pay taxes, claims, and administrative expenses. Make a final distribution near the close of the estate.

III.   Closing the Estate

_____ Apply for a discharge as an executor if the estate owes taxes and must file a return. As executor, you are personally liable for the payment of taxes. This is a request to the IRS to determine if additional taxes are due. This should be done before making final distributions.

_____ Determine if a decedent's final income-tax return must be filed. If the amount of gross income is less than the required filing amount, do not file a return unless the decedent has an overpayment of tax due him. Write "(DECEASED)" after the name at the top of the form and sign as executor. If a state income-tax refund is due the decedent, check with the local revenue office for forms to complete.

# The Accountant

The accountant's role in the administration of an estate is, generally, providing an accurate list of assets and liabilities. The accountant has expertise in determining the extent and value of the decedent's property. Depending on the size of an estate, there could be numerous state and federal tax forms that must be filed. Estimated tax payments must be made, trust returns filed, final income-tax returns prepared, and the complicated estate-tax returns filed. There are numerous elections to be considered, such as disclaimers. An accountant should be retained to calculate the lowest possible overall tax burden for the estate and the beneficiaries.

# Checklist for Accountants

(The following is a list of steps the accountant may follow in closing an estate. Additional steps may be needed for your estate, such as necessary to satisfy a specific state law requirement.)

1.      Preliminary Steps

_____   Obtain a copy of the death certificate to confirm date of death for time requirements for filing returns and obtaining any disclaimers.

_____   Check that decedent's last income-tax returns have been filed, and if any returns are under examination.

_____   Apply for a Federal Employer Identification Number from the Internal Revenue Service (Form SS-4) if the estate is required to file a Form 1041, U.S. Income Tax Return for Estates and Trusts. Form 1041 is required if the estate has gross income of $600 or more for the tax year, or a beneficiary who is a non-resident alien.

_____  Check if a state estate-tax return must be filed even though a federal return may not be required. If the decedent had real property in more than one state, check the filing requirements for each state.

II.       Administration of the Estate

_____  Review the estate inventory. Check for items that may be missing, including property over which the decedent may have had a power of appointment, insurance policies, prior transfers for less than fair market value, reversionary interests, and other.

_____  Scan the values listed for property for reasonableness. If the estate contains personal items with artistic value in excess of $3,000, obtain a written appraisal and attach to the estate Form 706 along with the appraiser's qualifications.

_____  If the decedent owned a closely held business, you will need to obtain a valuation from qualified appraisers and include five years of financial statements. Review Revenue Ruling 59-60 for information regarding acceptable evaluation techniques.

_____  Review the appraisal of the business. Does the appraised value seem realistic? Did the appraiser follow Revenue Ruling 59-60 in making the appraisal? Also, check if the appraiser considered the following items that may have to be taken into account to reach the true economic value of the business:

• Does the company have related party leases?
• Were there nonrecurring or extraordinary items of income that should not be taken into account in valuing the business?
• Was the compensation of key officers motivated by business performance or tax purposes?
• Are there pending lawsuits?
• Are there unrecorded tax liabilities or unfunded pension plans?
• Were there related party transactions?
• Are the assets valued at cost or market value?
• Did the appraiser take minority discounts if valuing stock?

_____ If this is a closely held business and the value of the stock exceeds 35 percent of the value of the adjusted gross estate, have you discussed Internal Revenue Code §303 stock redemptions with the executor? This section may allow the business to buy the stock without the estate being charged with dividend income.

_____ If this is a large estate and the executor wishes to dispose of personal property prior to an audit by the IRS, obtain the consent of the local IRS district director pursuant to Treasury Regulation 26 C.F.R. 20.2031(c).

_____ Determine if estimated tax payments are required for any trusts or the estate.

_____ If the estate property contains a *qualified family-owned business interest,* check if the requirements are met to claim the exclusion to decrease the size of the estate. (The requirements for the qualified family-owned business are listed in chapter 9 under Schedule T. The requirements include that the business owned by the decedent must exceed 50 percent of the adjusted gross estate.)

_____ Determine if the spouse should file disclaimers of property in order to fund any trusts included in the estate plan and take advantage of the decedent's unified credit exclusion. Make sure the spouse files a written disclaimer within nine months of date of death and prior to taking control over the property.

_____ Determine if any beneficiaries should file disclaimers of property in order to decrease the amount of taxes. Beneficiaries are allowed to disclaim property and later accept gifts in the amount of the disclaimer, provided the gifts are not actual consideration for the disclaimer.

_____ Determine if the estate should elect the *alternate valuation date* for property per Internal Revenue Code 2032. The alternate valuation is the fair market value, six months after the date of death, of property that has not been disposed of or transferred. This is an irrevocable election.

_____ If the decedent had a qualified intervivos trust (living trust), determine if an election should be made under (new) Internal Revenue Code 645 to elect to report the trust income as part of the estate rather than filing separate trust returns. The election must be made by the time for filing the estate-tax return. This is an irrevocable election. See Revenue Procedure 98-13, Internal Revenue Bulletin No. 1998-4 dated January 26, 1998, for how to make the election.

_____ If the estate has tax-exempt income, you must allocate a percentage of the administration expenses (legal and accounting fees) to the tax-exempt income. The allocated amount of legal and accounting fees are then nondeductible on the Form 1041. Calculate if the administration expenses should be claimed on the Form 706 instead of the Form 1041.

_____ If the value of a closely held business exceeds 35 percent of the adjusted gross estate, consider making the 6166 election to pay the estate tax in installments. Make this election on a timely filed Form 706.

_____ Determine if the surviving spouse was named beneficiary on the decedent's IRA account and, if yes, advise the spouse on the income-tax advantages of rolling over the account into her own IRA account.

_____ Check if any generation-skipping transfer elections can and should be made on any transfers to grandchildren or trusts for their benefit.

_____ Check if any generation-skipping transfer tax forms must be filed for distributions to beneficiaries more than one generation below the decedent.

III.    Closing the Estate

_____ Prepare final income-tax returns to pay taxes due or claim refunds.

_____ Prepare and file estate-tax returns with Forms 712, appraisals, trust agreements, financial statements, and explanations attached.

# Checklist for Attorneys (Independent Administration)

(The following is a list of steps an attorney may follow in handling an estate. Additional steps may be needed for your estate, such as necessary to satisfy a specific state law requirement or to obtain a court's ruling on a trust or will provision.)

I.     Preliminary Steps

_____ Send engagement letter and agreement to the executor. Discuss fee arrangements and what aspects of the estate each party will complete.

_____ Obtain a copy of and read all wills, amendments, trust agreements, and financial documents. Obtain a copy of the death certificate. Check office files for original will and trusts.

_____ Establish control sheets for estate administration with dates and responsible parties identified. List estimated-tax payment dates, return-filing dates, last date spouse may disclaim property, and creditor cutoff dates.

_____ Notify anyone who may have an adverse interest in the estate that you represent the executor and they should obtain their own legal counsel.

_____ Obtain background information on the decedent, such as names, ages, and dates of previous spouses, divorces, and children.

_____ Obtain copy of estate inventory and final Form 1040.

II.    Administration of the Estate (Illinois)

_____ File petition for letters of administration or office.

_____ Obtain a *surety bond* (if not waived by the will) and, if required, for one and two times the value of personal property in the estate.

_____ Place case on docket and appear in court to obtain letters of office for executor; present estate inventory, security bond, *affidavit of heirship, order declaring heirship, oath of office,* and *order admitting will to probate and appointing representative.*

_____ Publish notice in local newspaper.

_____ Notify all known creditors and beneficiaries named in the will.

_____ Request the court to approve guardians for minors if necessary.

_____ Accompany client to inventory safe-deposit boxes if requested.

_____ Order a title search on real property owned by the decedent, and review.

_____ Request a claim kit from each insurance company. Complete the applications, send a copy of the death certificate, and request a Form 712, Life Insurance Statement, for estate-tax filing purposes from each company. Insurance companies will request that you complete a Form W-9, Request for Taxpayer Identification Number and Certification; otherwise they must withhold for federal taxes.

_____ Review the estate inventory. Determine if there are any individuals who may have estate property that has not been turned over to the administrator. If yes, send a letter to the person requesting an explanation. Check if a citation to discover assets proceeding may be warranted.

_____ Pay spouse and child awards if applicable.

_____ Determine if ancillary probate is needed in another state and if yes, notify the executor and contact an attorney in the second state to begin proceedings.

_____ Determine distribution amounts and secure receipts.

_____ File a release of the estate's interest for real property with the county recorder's office if the property is not transferred prior to closing the estate.

_____ Review and pay legitimate claims if the executor has requested you to perform this function.

_____ Check with the accountant that all federal and state income and estate tax returns have been filed and taxes paid if necessary. Perform a cursory review of the estate tax returns. Are the decedent's final wages included in the estate tax return? Are there appraisals attached for personal property in excess of $5,000 in value? Were the correct boxes checked in making any QTIP election?

_____ Ensure that all property that is not subject to probate, such as held in trusts, is properly transferred.


III.     Closing the Estate

_____ Mail notice of final report to each beneficiary.

_____ Prepare and file final report and final accounting with court.

_____ File petition for discharge of administrator/executor.

_____ Send estate administration closing letter to client explaining services performed, and a copy of the final bill, if not already paid.

# Federal Income Tax Issues

T here are many tax issues that impact older taxpayers more than the rest of the population. Older citizens may have accumulated significant amounts in an individual retirement account and have reached the age where distributions must be made. Choosing the right beneficiary and distribution elections can decrease the amount of taxes paid and increase the opportunity for tax-deferred growth of the account over your beneficiary's lifetime. Decisions made when retiring from a company will affect the amount of taxes you or your beneficiaries pay in the long term. Retired taxpayers may have accumulated significant amounts in deferred compensation plans, have vacation homes they hope will remain in the family, may consider moving to a different state with a warmer climate, have higher medical expenses, and face other issues different from the younger generation's. It is always best to check with a competent financial advisor when a significant event occurs in your life, such as retirement or change of your permanent residence. This chapter explains some of the issues you may wish to consider in your estate planning.

## Points to Consider

- The Taxpayer Relief Act of 1997 changed the tax advantages for the sale of a primary residence.
- You must start withdrawing from your individual retirement account (IRA) by April 1 of the year following the year in which you turn age 70½. You may start withdrawing funds without penalty at age 59½.

• If you wish to decrease the size of your estate through gifts, realize that gifts of different types of property will have different consequences for both the donor and the donee.

• The form in which you decide to take remuneration from your company's retirement plan will affect the income taxes you pay.

## Primary Residences

The one-time exclusion of gain of up to $125,000 from the sale of principal residence by an individual who has attained age 55—Internal Revenue Code §121—was replaced with a new provision by the Taxpayer Relief Act of 1997 for home sales after May 6, 1997. The exclusion for home sales after May 6, 1997, is $250,000 ($500,000 for a married couple filing jointly), provided you owned and occupied the home as your principal residence in two out of the five preceding years. This exclusion may be used more than once, and a person's age does not matter. When an administrator or executor is reviewing real property owned by a decedent, she should establish how the decedent acquired his interest in the property. If the decedent paid no consideration for the property—let's say his spouse, who owned the property, simply put his name on the title for probate-avoidance purposes—the property should not be included in his estate.

## Individual Retirement Accounts

An individual retirement account (IRA) is often the single largest asset owned by a taxpayer. If the correct beneficiary designations and elections are made, the IRA owner and her beneficiaries can extend the life of the IRA over their joint life expectancies taking advantage of the minimum-distribution rules. For example, the IRA owner can designate his son as the beneficiary of the IRA and elect to have the distributions calculated over their joint life expectancies. This allows the account to grow tax deferred for a greater number of years, thereby increasing the value of the account. However, if the IRA owner designates a charity, his estate, or a nonqualifying trust as the beneficiary, only the owner's life expectancy can be used to calculate the distribution amount each year. In addition, if the owner's spouse is named as beneficiary of the IRA, the account will not be subject to federal estate taxes upon the owner's death. As stated above, a taxpayer must start withdrawing from his IRA by April 1 of the year following the year in which the taxpayer turns age 70½. A person may start withdrawing funds without penalty at age 59½. Distributions may be made from an IRA account prior to age 59½ without penalty for the following reasons:

- The distribution was to a beneficiary (or to the estate of the employee) on or after the death of the employee.
- The employee became disabled and is entitled to distribution.
- If the distribution is made as part of a series of substantially equal periodical payments (not less frequently than annually) made for the life (or life expectancy) of the employee or the joint lives (or joint life expectancies) of such employee and his designated beneficiary.
- Distributions made to pay medical expenses to the extent such expenses exceed 7.5 percent of adjusted gross income.
- If the IRA owner has been unemployed and receiving federal or state unemployment compensation for twelve consecutive weeks, and to pay health-insurance premiums for such unemployed individual.
- To pay for qualified higher education expenses of the owner, spouse, child, or grandchild.
- Distribution of up to $10,000 for first-time home purchases.

There are different methods for calculating the required minimum distributions from an IRA account. The owner may choose between term-certain, a recalculation method whereby you calculate an amount each year, or a hybrid method. Ask your accountant or financial advisor to explain which method will produce the lowest possible tax consequences for you. Since there are severe penalties for not taking the minimum distribution from the IRA after you reach age 70, check with your tax accountant regarding the calculation of distributions. Since a regular IRA has different tax consequences from a Roth IRA, make sure you know what type of account you are discussing with your accountant. In general, contributions to a regular IRA account are tax deductible at the time they are made, and the distributions are subject to income taxes, while contributions to a Roth IRA are not deductible but the distributions are not subject to income tax.

In some cases, it is advisable for a designated beneficiary to disclaim an IRA account to save federal estate taxes. For example, husband and wife name each other as the beneficiary of their respective IRA accounts. They are killed in a car accident, with the wife passing away first. The husband passes away a few days later. Since the wife passed away first, the husband inherits his wife's IRA account estate-tax-free due to the unlimited marital deduction. The husband's beneficiaries, their children, receive both the husband's and the wife's IRA accounts. In this case, the wife did not utilize her unified credit amount. The husband's estate can disclaim the wife's IRA account. The IRA then goes back into her estate and is distributed to her beneficiaries, the children. However, this allows her executor to claim the unified credit exclusion on her IRA, decreasing estate taxes and distributing a greater amount to the children.

## Gifts

One method of decreasing the size of any estate is simply to gift away the property. Since each person may gift away up to $10,000 in property each year per recipient without affecting his unified credit amount, making gifts to beneficiaries will decrease the amount of estate taxes due on death, thereby increasing the amount transferred to beneficiaries overall. When making gifts, however, there are a few issues that need to be considered.

First, property interest transferred needs to be a present interest, not a future interest, in order to qualify for the annual exclusion. For example, if you gift stock to a grandchild, you must actually transfer the stock, not make a promise to transfer the stock in the future. Second, in general, gifts made within three years of the date of death are brought back into the estate for estate-tax purposes. Try to start a gifting program to your beneficiaries at an early date to decrease the overall estate-tax burden.

Third, if you are transferring passive activity property (such as rental property), check with your tax accountant prior to making the gift. Since the amount of passive losses an individual may deduct on his income tax return is limited each year, some taxpayers have suspended tax losses carried over from prior years. These unused tax losses will be added to the donee's basis rather than allowed as a current deduction for the donor. Passive income includes interest and dividends earned, and distributions from partnerships and other businesses where the taxpayer is not an active participant. If you are making different gifts of equal value to various beneficiaries, consider gifting the rental property to the beneficiary who has sufficient passive income to use the losses in the future. Also, if you have been offsetting passive income from interest and dividends with losses from the rental properties, you may increase your current income taxes, since you will lose the benefit of the rental losses.

Fourth, if possible, do not gift away stock that has decreased in value. The person who receives the stock by gift has a tax basis in the stock equal to lower of market or the donor's basis. It is far better to sell the stock, deduct the capital loss, and gift the proceeds. For example, I purchased a hundred shares of ABC stock for $25,000. The stock has a current value of $10,000. If I gift the stock to my son, he receives a tax basis in the stock of $10,000 (not the $25,000 I paid.) If the stock increases in value to $15,000, and my son sells the stock, he will pay capital gains (income taxes) on the $5,000, since his basis in the stock is $10,000. Instead of gifting the stock, I should have sold the stock for $10,000, deducted a capital loss of $15,000 on my income tax return, and gifted the proceeds of $10,000 to my son.

Fifth, consider gifting away ownership of life-insurance policies. If you retain ownership or control of the policies, the proceeds will be included in your estate. Also, the current value of term policy may be almost nothing, which means it will be within the annual exclusion amount for gift purposes.

## Distributions from Employer Retirement Plans

Many employees who work for large corporations have accumulated a sizeable amount of company stock in the company's retirement plan. When retiring, consider NOT rolling over the stock (if highly appreciated in value) into an IRA account. While you may have to pay a 10 percent penalty for early withdrawal on the cost basis of the company stock, when you later sell the stock you will pay tax at the capital-gains rate on the profit, not the ordinary income tax rate. If the company stock is rolled over into an IRA, you will pay taxes at ordinary income-tax rates on the entire profit when distributions are made. This could be hundreds of thousands of dollars in tax savings over the long term. If you die with the appreciated stock in your IRA, the beneficiary will still have to pay tax at the higher ordinary income-tax rates due to the income-in-respect-of-a-decedent rules.

## Decedent Tax Forms

There is a number of IRS forms and federal taxes that may need to be paid in respect to a decedent. Depending upon the amount of money in the estate and the form of estate planning practiced by the decedent, different requirements will have to be met. Various financial plan options will have positive or negative consequences for both the estate and the beneficiaries, depending upon the nature of the estate. Before looking at what some of the options are, look at the following taxes and tax forms an estate may be responsible for:

*Form 1040 (of the decedent).*   Decedent's final U.S. Individual Income Tax Return Form 1040, required to be filed by April 15 of the following year. If the decedent died February 10, before filing his return for the preceding year, the preceding year must be filed. The final income-tax return will be for the period January 1 through February 10 of the year of death.

*Form 1040 (of the Beneficiary).*   The beneficiary must report any income in respect of a decedent that he received from the estate on his Form 1040.

*Form 706.*   Estate (and Generation-Skipping Transfer) Tax Return required to be filed nine months after date of death if gross assets plus gifts exceed the applicable exclusion amount ($675,000 in 2000).

*Form 1041 (filed by estate fiduciary).*   Estate's income-tax return required to be filed if estate's gross income exceeds $600 (in 1997); due the 15th day of the 4th month following the close of the tax year.

Form 1040 is no different from the form you file annually. Form 706, United States Estate (and Generation-Skipping Transfer) Tax Return is forty-four pages long and very complex. Chapter 10 goes into some detail concerning the filing of Form 706, but you will probably want professional assistance. Form 1041 U.S. Income Tax Return for Estate and Trusts, and all other tax forms mentioned can be easily accessed and downloaded at the forms page of the official IRS Web site, *www.irs.gov/forms_pubs/forms.html.*

## Income and Deductions in Respect of a Decedent

All gross income, wages, commissions, royalties, interest, deferred compensation, that a decedent would have reported on his income-tax return had death not occurred and had he collected the money is called "income in respect of a decedent (IRD)." An IRD is a receivable that the decedent had earned prior to death and would have collected. Since individuals report income on a cash basis, if a decedent did not receive money, check or cash, prior to his death, the income is taxed to the estate or person receiving the money. The unpaid, accrued amounts are also included on the estate Form 706 if the estate is required to file a return. If the accrued income is taxed twice (on the Form 706 and recipient's income-tax return, either Forms 1040 or 1041), the recipient is allowed a deduction for the estate tax attributable to this income.

The character of income to be reported by the beneficiary on his Form 1040 is by reference to its character in the hands of the decedent. If an item of income was long-term capital gain to the decedent, then it is long-term capital gain to the beneficiary.

The author does not wish to appear insensitive, but if death is certain in the near future, there are opportunities for tax planning. Certain losses, such as individual capital loss carryovers, cannot be claimed by either the estate or beneficiaries. That is, capital loss carryovers, which could have been claimed on a decedent's Form 1040 while he was alive, cannot be claimed by either the estate or the beneficiaries. Therefore, the decedent should try to maximize capital gains before he dies, in order to offset the fact that his estate and beneficiaries will not be able to take advantage of capital loss carryovers. Certain expenses may be deducted on more than one return.

If the executor satisfies *pecuniary legacies* of the will with IRD items, the estate will generate taxable income prior to collection of the receivable. Executors should attempt to transfer IRD items to charitable organizations, since they are generally tax exempt.

If the estate pays income taxes on an income item, the beneficiary receives a tax deduction for the taxes paid. Since a Form W-2 or 1099 will be forwarded to the IRS service center by the person paying the money, the IRS will want to match up the amount on an income-tax return.

EXAMPLE    John Smith died March 15. He had earned wages of $4,500 from January 1 to March 15, 1997. When he died, he had earned two weeks' salary that had not been paid, in the amount of $750. John's employer paid the $750 to his daughter, who was his only heir. John's executor will report $4,500 in wages on John's final 1040 and will report $750 on the Form 706 (if required to be filed). John's daughter will report $750 on her 1040. On her 1040, John's daughter should deduct the tax attributable to the $750 reported on Form 706.

EXAMPLE    Ed Jones died April 15. He had earned commissions in the amount of $14,500 from January 1 to April 15. When he died, he had earned commissions that had not been paid, in the amount of $6,000. Ed's employer paid the $6,000 to the executor of Ed's estate. The $14,500 paid to Ed before he died will be reported on his final

1040 form. The executor will report $6,000 in commissions on the fiduciary income tax return (1041) and will include $6,000 on the Form 706 (if required to be filed).

## ACCELERATED DEATH BENEFITS
If a terminally ill patient sells or assigns his right to a life-insurance policy with a viatical settlement provider, the benefits received on the policy are excluded from income.

## ACCRUED VACATION PAY
Companies often give accrued vacation pay to the spouses of deceased employees. The amount would be reported as income on the spouse's 1040. The income was earned by the decedent while alive, therefore it is a receivable that will have to be reported as income. If not reported by the spouse, the income should be reported on either the Fiduciary 1041 or Beneficiary 1040 (whoever received the money), with the full amount reported on the Estate 706. Accrued vacation pay of the decedent is not subject to employment taxes.

## ADMINISTRATION EXPENSES
Accounting and legal fees attributable to the estate are deductible on either the Estate 706 or Fiduciary 1041, but not both. If expenses exceed income on the Fiduciary 1041, they cannot be carried forward and are lost; an exception exists for the final Fiduciary 1041 when the losses are distributed to the beneficiaries. If deducted on the Form 1041, attach a statement to the Estate 706 that no administration expenses are deducted.

If the estate has tax-exempt income, it must allocate a percentage of administration expenses to the tax-exempt income, and that percentage is nondeductible on the Form 1041. If the estate has significant tax-exempt bonds, consider deducting the administration expenses on the Estate 706.

## BUSINESS INCOME
If the decedent was a cash-basis taxpayer, include sales and expenses on the Decedent 1040 for amounts actually received and paid prior to death. Amounts not received or paid prior to death are reported by either the Fiduciary 1041 or Beneficiary 1040. If the decedent was on the accrual basis, all income and expenses would be reported on the Decedent 1040, and not reflected on either the Fiduciary 1041 or Beneficiary 1040.

## CAPITAL GAINS AND LOSSES

Report capital gains and losses on the Decedent 1040 when payment was received prior to death. If payment is received after death, report on Fiduciary 1041 or Beneficiary 1040 and Estate 706. Capital loss carry-forwards can only be deducted on the Decedent 1040 and if not used up are lost forever, the same as net-operating loss carry forwards.

## CROP SHARES

A cash method farmer who receives rent in the form of crop shares or livestock and owns the rent at the time of death has income in respect of a decedent for the amount of rent or crop shares earned up to the date of death. The number of days in the rent period is divided by the number of days alive to determine the percentage of income reported by the farmer. The remainder is reported by the estate or beneficiary. The full amount is included on the Estate 706.

## DEATH-BENEFIT-ONLY PLANS

Generally, lump-sum distributions from deferred compensation plans from an employer are included in the decedent's gross estate pursuant to §2039(b). If an employer pays a death benefit to the spouse, however, and the decedent never had a right to the amount while he was alive, the amount may be excluded from the gross estate.

## DEFERRED COMPENSATION

Deferred-compensation plans, such as 401(k), paid directly to a beneficiary are includible in the income-tax return of the beneficiary. See the discussion under Individual Retirement Accounts below. The full amount is included on the Estate 706.

## DIVIDENDS

While uncashed dividend checks are reported on the final income-tax return of the decedent, since he had received the funds prior to death, dividends declared prior but paid after date of death are reported by the recipient (Beneficiary 1040 or Fiduciary 1041). The full amount is included on the Estate 706.

## EDUCATION IRA

The balance in an education individual retirement account must be distributed within thirty days after death. If the decedent's estate receives the income, the amount is reported on the decedent's final Form 1040. If a beneficiary receives the balance, they report the income on their Form 1040. It would also go on Estate 706 (if required to be filed).

## FUNERAL AND RELATED EXPENSES

Funeral and related expenses cannot be deducted on the Decedent 1040, but generally are deducted on the Estate 706. If liability for paying the expenses passes to a beneficiary as a result of a transfer of property, the expenses may be deducted on the Beneficiary 1040.

## INCOMPLETE SALES OF PROPERTY

Amounts actually received prior to death are reported on the Decedent 1040. Amounts received after death are reported by either the Fiduciary 1041 or Beneficiary 1040, whoever collects the money. The income is reported with the same characteristics, capital gains or ordinary income, as the decedent would have reported.

## INDIVIDUAL RETIREMENT ACCOUNTS

If the decedent was already receiving distributions from his IRA account, the beneficiary must receive the distributions at least as quickly as the decedent would have received them. See Internal Revenue Code §408(a)(6) referencing §401(a)(9). The full amount is included on the Estate 706, unless the spouse is named as beneficiary.

 If the surviving spouse is the beneficiary, the decedent's account may be rolled over into the spouse's IRA or the spouse may leave the funds in the IRA without making distributions until the decedent would have reached age 70½. The surviving spouse may make deductible contributions to the account.

 If the beneficiary is not the surviving spouse, the account cannot be rolled over into the beneficiary's IRA account and the beneficiary cannot make deductible contributions to the account. The beneficiary must either take distributions from the account with the complete distribution within five years of date of death or distributions over the life expectancy of the beneficiary, provided the distributions begin within one year of date of death. The full amount in included on the Estate 706.

 An individual may name his living trust his IRA beneficiary. This may assist in deferring the amount of income tax paid in future years.

## INSTALLMENT SALES

If the decedent had sold property on the installment basis, use the decedent's gross profit percentage for calculating income. Follow the same procedure as incomplete sales above; amounts actually received prior to death are reported on the Decedent 1040. Amounts received after death are reported by either the Fiduciary 1041 or Beneficiary 1040, whoever collects the money. The income is reported with the same characteristics, capital gains or ordinary income, as the decedent would have reported.

## INTEREST ON SAVINGS ACCOUNTS

Interest income on the decedent's savings accounts earned up to the date of death is reported on the Decedent 1040 (the money was constructively paid to him). The Fiduciary 1041 reports the interest income from date of death to the distribution date, and the Beneficiary 1040 reports interest income from the date of distribution forward.

## LIFE INSURANCE PROCEEDS

Life insurance proceeds are not taxable income and therefore are not reported on the Decedent 1040, Fiduciary 1041, or Beneficiary 1040. The proceeds will be included on the Estate 706 if the decedent had an ownership interest in the policies. If the decedent was required to maintain a life insurance policy on himself made payable to a former spouse pursuant to a divorce decree, this will be considered a reversionary interest, and the proceeds will be included in the decedent's estate.

If the beneficiary elects to receive the proceeds of an insurance policy over a term of years, the principal is excluded each year with the remainder reported as interest income.

## MEDICAL AND DENTAL EXPENSES

Medical and dental expenses paid within one year of date of death can be claimed on either the Decedent 1040 or the Estate 706. Since medical and dental expenses are subject to the 7.5 percent AGI limitation on the 1040, compare which method will result in the lowest amount of tax due. The medical and dental expenses cannot be claimed on the Fiduciary 1041. If claimed on the Decedent 1040, attach a statement that the expenses have not been claimed by the estate.

## MEDICAL SAVINGS ACCOUNTS

Medical savings accounts (MSA) are treated similar to individual retirement accounts. If the decedent's spouse acquires the interest in the MSA, the account will be treated as owned by the spouse. See Internal Revenue Code §220(f)(8)(A). If decedent's estate becomes the owner, the fair market value of the account is included in the Decedent 1040. If someone other than the spouse becomes the owner, the account ceases to be an MSA and the fair market value of the account will be included in the owner's 1040. He is, however, entitled to a deduction under §691(c) for the amount of estate tax paid for the MSA account. If someone other than the surviving spouse pays medical expenses for the decedent within one year of the decedent's death, the amount of the MSA to be included in their income is reduced by the amount of the payments.

## NET OPERATING LOSS CARRYOVERS

Individual net operating loss carry-forwards of the decedent can only be deducted on the decedent's final 1040 and, if not used up, are lost forever.

## PARTNERSHIP INCOME/LOSS

If the partnership tax year ends prior to the date of death, include partnership income on the Decedent 1040. For example, if the partnership year ends June 30 and the decedent died August 31, the decedent's distributive share of the income and losses would be reported on his final income-tax return.

For partnership tax years beginning January 1, 20__, include the partner's share of income and losses up to the date of death. Previously, if the partnership tax year ended December 31, no portion of the partnership income would be reported on the decedent's final income-tax return, since partnership income or loss is considered earned on the last day of the partnership year (except for self-employment tax purposes). Whoever had the right to receive the income, either estate or beneficiary, would report the partnership income. If the spouse holds a successor in interest in the partnership, she will report the income and losses on her return (which may be filed as joint with the decedent). Include the distributive share of partnership income on the Estate 706.

## RENTAL INCOME AND EXPENSES

Report rental income and expenses the same as business income discussed previously. The basis for depreciation will change in the year following the death of the owner. The survivor or beneficiary will receive a stepped-up basis on the decedent's share of the property.

## ROTH IRA

If the decedent withdrew amounts from a traditional IRA account and rolled it over into a Roth IRA account and was reporting the taxable conversion over a four-year period, the remaining years of the taxable conversion must be reported for income-tax purposes. The spouse can report the remaining years of taxable conversion on her Form 1040 if she receives the account, otherwise, the remaining taxable conversion is reported on the decedent's final 1040.

## SALARY CONTINUATION PAYMENTS

If an employer voluntarily continues to pay a decedent's salary after the date of death, regardless of the fact the compensation was never earned by the decedent, the salary is income in respect of a decedent and is taxable to the recipient. The payments are not considered gifts. They would be reported on the Beneficiary 1040, but not the Estate 706, since there is no legally enforceable claim to the money.

## SELF-EMPLOYMENT INCOME

Report income actually received and the decedent's share of partnership income and losses prorated through the end of the month of death on the decedent's final 1040. You must file a final return for the decedent if he or she had self-employment income of $400 or more.

## STATE INCOME TAXES

State income tax on the Decedent 1040 can be deducted on both the Estate 706 and Fiduciary 1041.

## TAX PREPARATION FEES

Tax preparation fees attributable to the decedent's final income-tax return can be deducted on both the Estate 706 and Fiduciary 1041.

## U.S. SAVINGS BOND INTEREST

Accumulated U.S. savings bond interest may be reported on the decedent's final income-tax return, estate-tax return, or the beneficiary's income-tax return. Compare which method will result in the lowest amount of tax due. Bonds do not receive a stepped-up basis to fair market value on date of death as most other property. Report the redemption value at date of death on the Estate 706. If testator's will directs the bonds be left to a tax-exempt charity, the estate does not have to recognize the accrued interest income when transferring the bonds. See IRS PLR 9845026.

## WAGES

Wages earned and paid prior to death are reported on the decedent's final 1040. Accrued earnings not paid prior to death are included on the Estate 706. Since the decedent is a cash-basis taxpayer and did not receive the check prior to death, the wages are reportable by either the Fiduciary 1041 or Beneficiary 1040 if paid directly to them. The amount is included on the Estate 706. If the spouse receives the payment and files a joint income-tax return, it will end up on the Decedent 1040. Wages paid after date of death are not subject to employment taxes.

# Federal Estate Tax Planning

ederal estate and gift taxation is a highly complex subject that takes years of study to understand and requires continuing education to stay current with the law. This chapter is a very brief outline of selected topics. The estate-tax rates, which are included in the appendices, range from 37 to 55 percent. The graduated rates are phased out for estates larger than $10 million. The tax is based on the transfer of a person's property and is generally paid within nine months after the date of death. The estate tax should not be confused with income taxes, which are assessed on a person's income each year. The crucial question to remember is: did the person own or control the property on the date of his death? A person is considered an owner if the property is titled in his name; if he has a power of appointment over the property not subject to a contingency; if he makes gifts of property for the three years prior to his death; if he is the beneficiary of a living trust; if he has control over life-insurance policies; if he has a possibility of a reversionary interest; and other items. Remember that living trusts have no benefit for reducing estate taxes, since, by definition, a person controls property held in his living trust.

The Federal United States Estate (and Generation-Skipping Transfer) Tax Return, Form 706, must be filed for the estate of every U.S. citizen or resident if the fair market value of the gross estate exceeds $675,000 (2000 amount) or the decedent made taxable gifts after 1976 not included in the gross estate. The return must be filed nine months after the date of death.

A six-month extension may be granted for filing the return but not for paying the tax. There are limited exceptions for paying the tax in installments.

If your gross estate is less than the applicable threshold amount at death, you will owe no estate taxes, provided you haven't used up your unified credit (exclusion amount) in prior years by taxable gifts. There are numerous techniques available, which can reduce or freeze the size of your estate to help avoid or minimize the tax. Consult with a tax advisor as early as possible if you believe your estate may end up paying estate taxes.

When your gross estate is near the threshold amount, you may consider a program of gifting up to $10,000 ($20,000 between yourself and your spouse, if you are married) in property to each of your beneficiaries each year. This amount is indexed to inflation and is subject to increase in future years. If these same distributions are deferred until after your death, your beneficiaries may receive only 45 cents on the dollar due to taxes.

Some gifting techniques, such as transfers to a charitable remainder trust, also provide for a current income tax deduction.

## Points to Consider

- Apportionment of Tax. If there may be estate taxes due, review language in your will and trusts to determine who will pay the taxes. If there is a specific bequest to one person with the remainder of your estate to another, the second beneficiary will end up paying all the taxes.

- Generation-Skipping-Transfer Tax. There is an additional tax for transfers made to a generation below the decedent, such as to grandchildren, for amounts over $1,000,000. Each person has a $1,000,000 generation-skipping transfer (GST) exemption, which cannot be deferred. The exemption amount can be allocated between trusts. There is a predeceased child exclusion if a parent dies.

- Gifts. If made within three years of the date of death, they are brought back into the estate for tax purposes except when a gift-tax return was not required to be filed, not counting insurance policies. Gifts to corporations do not qualify for the annual exclusion.

- Inherited Property. If you inherit property from someone whose estate paid estate taxes within the past ten years (or if his estate paid taxes up to two years after *your* death if his property went to *your* estate), there is a credit on your estate taxes for a percentage of estate taxes previously paid on the property.
- Stepped-up Basis. Property owned by the decedent at date of death is given a stepped-up basis to fair market value. A stepped-up basis is not allowed if property was received by the decedent by gift within one year of death and the property reverts back to the donor. Generally, one half of jointly owned property is given a stepped-up basis, except for community property states. See IRS TAM 9308002, for property held in a joint trust.

> EXAMPLE    Tom Smith gifts to his father stock that has a fair market value of $100,000, which he purchased for $25,000. Tom's father dies six months later, and in his will he leaves the stock to Tom. The stock has a fair market value of $125,000 on the date of his death. Although beneficiaries would normally receive the stepped-up basis of $125,000 on the stock, since the stock reverts to Tom (the donor), his basis in the stock is the $25,000.

- Unified Credit. Each person is entitled to a unified credit of $220,550 against the gross estate tax (2000 amount). This $220,550 tax credit translates into $675,000 of property that is excluded from estate taxation. The schedule for increases in the credit amount is included in the Glossary. With minor exceptions, jointly owned property does not qualify. It is called a unified credit because it takes into account the gross value of the estate and taxable gifts made after 1976. If a person dies with all of his property held in joint tenancy, he may not use up the credit, which will be lost forever.
- Unlimited Marital Deduction. If both spouses are U.S. citizens, the first to die can transfer an unlimited amount of property to the other at death, with federal estate taxes deferred until the second spouse dies. One estate-planning method is to create a credit-shelter trust for the first $675,000 (2000 amount) of decedent's property (to take advantage of his unified credit) with the remainder of his property transferred to a marital deduction trust. This method prevents paying any estate taxes on the first to die. There cannot be any restrictions placed on the property in the marital deduction trust in order to qualify for the unlimited marital deduction.

# Techniques to Decrease Estate Taxes

The following are very brief descriptions of several methods available to reduce the impact of federal estate taxes and preserve the gross value of your estate for your beneficiaries. Some of these methods were described in chapter 4. Some methods may no longer be valid as a result of changes in laws or court decisions. There also may be state laws that you must consider when using some of these techniques. Check with your attorney and accountant when planning to reduce or freeze the size of your estate.

## BYPASS OR UNIFIED CREDIT-SHELTER TRUST

The use of a bypass or credit-shelter trust will take full advantage of your unified exemption amount and allow you to designate the beneficiaries. This trust is usually included in a living trust that allows the trustee to fund the trust. The spouse may have to file disclaimers in order to fully fund the trust. The trustee will have to obtain a federal identification number for the trust, since it becomes an irrevocable trust.

## CHARITABLE TRUSTS AND POOLED INCOME FUNDS

These are methods that you can use to fulfill your donative intentions, retain either an income stream or remainder interest in the property transferred, decrease the size of your estate for tax purposes and, in most cases, receive charitable income-tax deductions based on the present value of the remainder to the charity. You are allowed to be the initial trustee, but you can't change your mind and take the property back, since these are irrevocable trusts. Generally, the charity must be located in the United States to qualify. There are minimum distribution requirements, and the value of the interest to the charity must be above a certain percentage. Charitable organizations are generally tax exempt, but will pay fiduciary income tax on unrelated business taxable income. If the income beneficiary is a descendant more than one generation below the donor, watch for generation-skipping transfer-tax implications.

A charitable trust can split the current and remainder interests into separate parts and designate separate parties for the interests. Both private individuals and charitable organizations can be named in the trust. If a transfer to a charity is conditioned on a subsequent event or condition after the death of the grantor, a charitable deduction is allowed only if the possibility that the charity will not receive the property is remote. If the trustee is empowered to divert the property to other than charitable purposes, then a deduction is allowed for that portion only, not subject to the power unless the property was given to the charity. See Treasury Regulation 20 C.F.R. 20 §2055-2(b). Non-income-producing property, such as art works, can be placed into a charitable trust.

### CHARITABLE LEAD TRUST

Property is placed into an irrevocable trust either during the lifetime of grantor or at death with the trust income donated to a qualifying charity for a term of years, after which the remainder interest reverts to the grantor or others. Current income-tax deductions are not allowed to the grantor unless the grantor is taxed on the income of the trust. If beneficiaries are the recipients of the property at the end of the term, the value of the gift for estate-tax purposes is the present value on the date of transfer into the trust. Appreciation of the donated property, if any, will be kept out of the grantor's estate. The annual payout is equal to either a fixed percentage of the net assets at the inception of the trust *(charitable lead annuity trust)* or a fixed percentage of the net assets of the trust at the end of each year *(charitable lead unitrust)*.

### CHARITABLE REMAINDER TRUST

In order to qualify for a charitable tax deduction if a charity is to receive a remainder interest, a taxpayer must select either a charitable remainder annuity trust, a charitable remainder unitrust, or a *pooled-income fund*. Property is placed into an irrevocable trust with a qualifying charity designated as the beneficiary at trustor's death or the end of the trust term. Income from the trust is directed to either the trustor or a noncharitable beneficiary during the term of the trust, with the remainder transferred to a charity. This technique allows for a current income-tax charitable deduction for the trustor based on the present value of the gift (even though it will not be transferred to the charity until trustor's date of death). The annual payout is equal to either a fixed percentage of the net assets at the inception of the trust (charitable remainder annuity trust) or an amount determined by: (1) a fixed percentage of the net assets of the trust at the end of each year; or (2) the annual trust income (charitable remainder unitrust). Under a GRUT, the payout can be calculated by one of three methods: (1) a fixed percentage of the net assets of the trust valued annually; (2) the lesser of a fixed percentage of the net assets of the trust valued annually or the annual net income of the trust; or (3) an amount determined under the net income method (2). However, in any year where the trust income exceeds the fixed percentage amount, the excess trust income is paid to make up for payments in prior years, when the trust income was less than the fixed percentage method. The income-tax savings could be invested in life insurance, which could restore some of the amount of the gift for the beneficiaries. The remainder interest in property that is out of the country, for example, vacation homes in Switzerland, can be donated to a qualified charity, provided the law of the land where the property is located allows the remainder interest to be donated.

### POOLED-INCOME FUNDS

Certain qualified charitable organizations maintain pooled-income funds. A donor transfers property to the fund where the property is mixed with other donor's' funds. The donor makes an irrevocable transfer of the remainder interest in the fund to the charity. The donor names himself or another to receive the income during his lifetime from the fund. On the death of the donor, the charity receives the principal. The donor does not recognize gain or loss on transfer of property to the fund. A charitable deduction is allowed the donor. Pooled-income funds are described in Internal Revenue Code §642 (c)(5).

## FAMILY PARTNERSHIPS

This is a technique of placing ownership of property into a partnership with the parents designated as general partners and children as limited partners. The IRS allows parents to establish a partnership with their children (See IRS PLR 9415007 for an explanation). Each year the parents gift additional partnership interests to the children, which are considered valid gifts, since there is delivery of a present interest. Upon dissolution of the partnership, assets are distributed in accordance with the partner's capital interests. A family partnership allows management of family wealth to be controlled by the parents, until such time as they decide to transfer ownership. There are no independent trustees who charge fees or may bind the trust through their actions. The property does not require probate proceedings to be transferred. The benefits of stepped-up basis will be lost, however, so a family partnership is generally better for larger estates.

A family partnership provides asset protection from creditors or ex-spouses, and helps to avoid higher marginal estate-tax rates. A court ruling did place restrictions on the use of a family partnership as an estate-planning technique. If the general partner retains control over the partnership property, that property may be included in their estate per §2036(a)(1).

## GENERATION-SKIPPING TRANSFERS

Each person may transfer up to $1,000,000 to beneficiaries two genera-
tions below (for example, a grandfather to his grandchildren) without
imposition of additional generation-skipping transfer taxes. If you leave
$1,000,000 to your son who then passes away more than ten years later, his
estate will end up paying estate taxes on the $1,000,000 a second time.
When possible, leave the maximum GST exemption amount to your
grandchildren directly or in a trust for their benefit. The exemption
amount can be allocated between gifts or trusts. If you do not allocate the
exemption, make sure your executor or trustee has the authority in a trust
agreement or will to allocate the exemption.

If you have a QTIP trust and are leaving a significant amount of
property to your spouse, you may not utilize your generation-skipping
transfer exemption. Your executor may make what is called a reverse QTIP
election, so the property is treated as though it was passed from the decedent to the grandchildren and not to the spouse first.

## GIFTS

Each person may gift away up to $10,000 each to an unlimited number
of people each year without affecting their unified-credit amount. This
$10,000 amount will increase in future years due to inflation. Husbands
and wives together may gift away $20,000 to a single person every year.
The gifts must be for a present interest, not a future interest. The donee
inherits the lower of cost or fair market value on the date of gift. In
addition to the $10,000 per year, you may pay the educational (tuition)
and medical-care expenses of a person—if the payments are made
directly to the institution and not the individual—without affecting
your unified credit.

If you have income-tax-deferred property, such as an IRA or U.S.
savings bonds, and are planning on making charitable donations in your
will, consider specifically leaving the tax-deferred property to the charity
in lieu of other property. Since the tax-deferred property will result in
income in respect of a decedent to the recipient, leaving the tax-deferred
property to a charity, which generally does not pay income taxes, and the
other non-tax-deferred property to your beneficiaries will result in more
wealth to your heirs.

The Taxpayer Relief Act of 1997 restricts the revaluation of gifts by
the IRS after the applicable statute of limitations, when properly disclosed
on a gift-tax return.

Gifts to corporations do not qualify for the annual exclusion, since this is not a gift of a present interest. Gifts to trusts will qualify for the exclusion amount if: (1) the trust sends the *Crummey* notices to the beneficiaries each year; (2) the trust is required to distribute its income annually; or (3) a trust was created under §2503(c) of the Internal Revenue Code. The trusts covered under §2503(c) are explained below.

### GIFTS *CAUSA MORTIS*

These are gifts made in contemplation of death. They are not favored in state laws, but can be valid gifts. The main problems associated with gifts *causa mortis* are delivery and intent. A person on his death bed who tells a visitor that, if he should die, they ought to give his good friend Edmund his car, has neither actually made delivery of the gift (car), nor does he have present intentions to make a gift. He has made known his intentions regarding a possible future gift, with the contingency that he die. There are the problems of no delivery or intent. The car will be brought back into his estate for federal estate-tax purposes, since it was made within three years of the date of his death. Properly prepared and executed wills and trusts would avoid the potential litigation and animosity surrounding this gift.

### GIFTS TO MINORS

A §2503(c) trust permits gifts to minors (under age twenty-one), which qualify for the annual gift tax exclusion even though the beneficiary may not receive the property until she attains the age of twenty-one. If not for this section, the gifts would be for a future interest and therefore not qualify for the exclusion. The property must be distributed to the minor upon his reaching the age twenty-one. The regulations (§25.2503-4) provide the trust agreement must meet certain criteria, which include: (1) both the property and income may be disbursed for the benefit of the minor prior to age twenty-one; (2) the accumulated trust property must be distributed at age twenty-one; and (3) any portion of the trust not distributed prior to age twenty-one, if the donee dies, will be payable to the donee's estate or whomever the donee appoints. If you wish to defer the trust distribution until after age twenty-one, you may include language in the agreement for a §2503(b) trust. The income that is available and distributed to the donee each year will qualify for the annual gift-tax exclusion but the remaining principal of the trust is considered a future interest in property and does not qualify for the exclusion.

## IRREVOCABLE LIFE-INSURANCE TRUSTS

As described previously, this is a method of having an irrevocable trust own life-insurance policies, which effectively removes the proceeds from the decedent's gross estate. If a person dies owning a life-insurance policy, the proceeds are income-tax-free but included in the gross estate for estate-tax purposes. If a person transfers ownership of the policy to a trust at least three years prior to his death, the insurance proceeds are not taxed for federal estate-tax purposes. Life-insurance proceeds are brought back into the estate of the decedent if:

- They are payable to the executor or decedent.
- The insured had incidents of ownership in the policy at death.
- The ownership interest was transferred within three years of date of death.

An irrevocable life-insurance trust will remove insurance proceeds from the estate and provide cash, which can be used to pay taxes or replace the wealth lost to taxes. There is little, if any, difference between the use of an irrevocable life-insurance trust or transferring the ownership of the policies to one's children outright. The person setting up the trust can make gifts to the trust for insurance premiums, but the beneficiaries must have the right to withdraw the gift. This right to withdraw the gift is evidenced by a notice to them from the trustee of their right to withdraw the amounts within thirty to sixty days; this is known as *Crummey* powers.

## LIFE-INSURANCE POLICIES TRANSFERRED

If you are the owner of a $100,000 life-insurance policy on yourself at death, approximately $55,000 of the proceeds could go to the federal government in estate taxes. The owner of a policy should transfer ownership of the policy either to his children three years before date of death or to an irrevocable life-insurance trust and retain no incidents of ownership. Provided there are sufficient other assets to pay taxes, the full amount will go to the beneficiaries and not be included in the estate. Consider gifting away term insurance rather than whole life policies. The replacement value of a term policy for gift purposes is near $0 while whole life policies have a cash-surrender value. A term policy has a value near $0 until you die. A whole life policy with a cash value is valued at the cash value. In order to stay under the $10,000 annual exclusion for gifts, it is better to gift away term policies. If you must gift away insurance policies with a high cash-surrender value, consider borrowing against the policy (to decrease its value) prior to transferring, and gift the cash.

## MARITAL TRUST

A decedent's taxable estate is allowed a deduction for property that passes to the surviving spouse, provided there are no restrictions on the spouse's interest. Since the property will then be included in the second spouse's estate, the estate taxes are deferred until the second spouse dies. The trust used to receive the property is called a marital or an *A trust*. This is generally used in estate planning with a unified-credit shelter trust, sometimes called an AB trust. For property to qualify for the unlimited marital deduction under §2056 of the Internal Revenue Code, the spouse must have unlimited power over the property. If a trustee has the right to terminate a spouse's interest, the property will not qualify for the unlimited marital deduction. An exception is allowed for property placed into a qualified terminal interest property (QTIP) trust. In a QTIP trust, the spouse receives the income for her life but does not have power, except in limited circumstances, over the trust principal.

## MINORITY DISCOUNTS IN CLOSELY HELD CORPORATIONS

The subject of acceptable stock valuations is complex and beyond the scope of this book. If a decedent has a minority interest in a closely held company rather than complete ownership, decedent's minority interest will result in a lower value of the stock for federal estate- and gift-tax purposes, since the minority interest has less control in the corporation. It will not matter for lower valuation purposes if the minority interest passes to a child holding the remainder of the interests. See Letter Ruling 9432001. In your estate-planning discussions, talk with your accountant about transferring partial interests in your closely held companies to your children during your lifetime. There are also discounts for lack of marketability of stock.

## PRIVATE FOUNDATIONS

Some wealthy individuals with charitable intentions establish private foundations that make grants to charitable organizations. Although there is no minimum dollar amount required to establish a private foundation, due to excise taxes and distribution requirements, only the very wealthy should consider this type of charitable contribution. Income-tax deductions for cash donations to a private foundation are limited to 30 percent of a taxpayer's adjusted gross income (AGI), gifts of appreciated stock are deductible at fair market value up to 20 percent of AGI, and other property must first be reduced by the amount of long-term capital gain that would have been reported. Bequests in a will to the private foundation have no limitations.

## QUALIFIED PERSONAL-RESIDENCE TRUST (QPRT)

This method allows parents to transfer a personal residence or vacation home into a trust and retain a life estate with the remainder to their children. Since the parents retain a present interest, the value of the property passing to the children is reduced for estate-tax purposes. There are specific provisions that must be included in the agreement in order to qualify. See Treasury Regulation 26 C.F.R. §25.2702-5(c).

## QUALIFIED TERMINAL-INTEREST PROPERTY TRUST (QTIP)

This estate-planning method allows a decedent to provide income for a spouse for life but directs the disposition of the property at that spouse's death. Although it is the executor who makes the election to consider property as QTIP, the trust agreement must be drafted prior to the decedent's death. This is an excellent protective technique for children from a first marriage. The spouse must have the right to all of the income on the property for her life and receive it at least annually. No person can have the power during her life to appoint any part of the property to any other person. You can create and fund a QTIP during your lifetime, which provides asset protection from creditors, with certain exceptions, but you will lose control over the property. A spouse's creditors are able to attach the income stream from the QTIP. Property transferred to a QTIP is eligible for an estate tax deduction on the decedent's return (Internal Revenue Code §2056(b)(7)) and included in the estate of the spouse (Internal Revenue Code §2044(b)) The disadvantage to a QTIP is that the property may appreciate in value, resulting in higher estate taxes when the second spouse dies.

## REVERSE QTIP ELECTION

This is not an estate-planning method, but an option that can be used by the executor or trustee after the death of a decedent when he has not utilized his entire generation-skipping transfer (GST) exemption amount. The typical estate plan used by married couples includes a will with a credit-shelter trust for the first $675,000 of decedent's property, with the remainder transferred to a QTIP trust. This technique defers estate taxes when the first spouse dies. It does not, however, use up the decedent's $1,000,000 GST exemption when the estate has significant wealth. In order to take advantage of the exemption, Internal Revenue Code §2652(a)(3), (known as a reverse QTIP election) allows the estate to make an election to treat the property as though the QTIP election was not made for this property. This will use up the remaining amount of the GST exemption. The election is made on Schedule R of the Form 706.

## SALES OF PROPERTY

One method of decreasing the size of your estate is to sell your property. Sales must be for fair market value or the difference may be considered a gift. Sales of shares of a closely held company may result in a disproportionate decrease in the value of the remaining shares, thereby reducing the size of the estate. Installment sales of remainder interests may assist beneficiaries with limited assets. If you own a corporation, you may consider executing a buy/sell agreement with your corporation for your shares to be purchased from your estate. Provided the redemption value of the shares is reasonable, this will ease the administration of your estate and possibly lower taxes. You may consider installment sales to your children to reduce the size of your estate. You could use the annual gift-tax exclusion amount—$10,000—to forgive part or all of the installment payment due each year. You would have to report interest income on your individual income-tax return each year.

## SELF-CANCELING INSTALLMENT NOTE (SCIN)

A SCIN is similar to a private annuity, transfer of property for an installment obligation, but with one major difference. With a SCIN, the *annuitant* transfers property to a third party pursuant to a written agreement that provides payments stop at a fixed term or upon the death of the annuitant (fixed term which is less than expected life of annuitant). The canceled obligation is not considered income in respect of a decedent but is included on the decedent's final income-tax return. Since the installment payments cease upon death, the obligation has no remaining value and therefore will not be included in the decedent's gross estate.

> EXAMPLE     Father, age 62, transfers to his son $100,000 in property in exchange for a SCIN (which provides that any unpaid obliga-

tion is canceled upon the death of father). The son's obligation is $11,000 per year for ten years, consisting of principle of $10,000 and interest of $1,000. Since this is not a gift, no gift-tax return is required. Father retains no security interest in the property. Son pays $11,000 per year. Father includes $1,000 in interest each year on his individual income-tax return. Father dies four years later when the remaining obligation is $60,000. On son's income-tax return, $60,000 is treated as income under Internal Revenue Code §61(a)(12); father's estate does not include the $60,000 on the estate-tax return. Son's basis in the property is $100,000.

## UNIFORM TRANSFERS TO MINORS ACTS

Every state has enacted some version of the Uniform Transfers to Minors Act. Parents with large estates should take advantage of the annual gift exclusion and transfer money into minor accounts. However, if the donor (parent) dies before the minor reaches the age of majority, the entire value is brought back into the decedent's estate. Unearned income for children less than fourteen years of age is taxed at the marginal rate of their parents. Transferring funds to minors may become disadvantageous later, when the children apply for financial aid for college.

# 10

# Federal Estate and Gift Tax

The U.S. estate (and generation-skipping transfer) tax return—Form 706—is used to compute the tax imposed by chapters 11 and 13 of the Internal Revenue Code. The form consists of forty-one pages of schedules and instructions and applies to the transfer of property at death. If the estate fails to pay the tax, each beneficiary may be held liable for any taxes due up to the amount of their share of the estate received. The Form 706 must be filed by the executor on or before nine months since the date of death if:

- The value of (adjusted) taxable gifts made after 12/31/76 plus the total of gifts allowed under §2521 (section that was repealed in 1976) for gifts made after 9/8/76 plus the gross value of decedent's estate at the date of death is more than $675,000 (2000 amount).

- The gross estate includes all property the decedent had an interest in, including property held outside the United States. The decedent's property and debts are listed on the tax return in schedules provided.

---

**CAUTION**

Certain elections must be made within nine months from the date of decedent's death, such as the election for qualified terminal-interest property and qualified disclaimers. While extensions to pay the tax can be obtained, a timely filed estate-tax return is a must. When in doubt, contact a competent tax advisor at the earliest opportunity.

---

# Points to Consider

• The U.S. estate (and generation-skipping transfer) tax return, Form 706, is a very complicated tax return that must be signed by all executors. There are penalties for late filing and underpayment of tax. I highly recommend finding a tax advisor to complete and file when applicable.

• If you overpay the amount of estate tax due and file a claim for refund, the IRS will not pay interest on the overpayment. This is different from overpayments of income taxes where interest is refunded.

• The valuation of closely held companies can be very difficult with minority discounts and lack-of-marketability discounts. Hire qualified appraisers.

• The 15 percent penalty for excess accumulations and excess distributions from qualified retirement accounts was repealed by the Taxpayer Relief Act of 1997. This excise tax was in addition to income taxes. An excess distribution in a calendar year was considered to be the greater of $155,000 or a lump sum of $755,000, for which the taxpayer elected five or ten year averaging.

• Deferral of Estate Tax. If 35 percent of the value of the estate consists of an interest in a closely held business, the estate may make an election to defer the initial payment of the estate tax due attributable to the business for up to five years, payable in installments up to ten years. Interest, at a new reduced rate, is due annually but is no longer deductible. See Treasury Regulation 20.6166-1(b) for election procedure.

• Special Use Valuation. Up to $750,000 in farming real property and closely held business real property may be excluded from federal estate taxation. The 1997 tax act allows an exclusion for family-owned business interests.

# Filing Form 706

If the testator dies with a valid will, a certified copy of the will should be attached to the return. A copy of the death certificate also must be attached. Life insurance statements, Forms 712, gift-tax returns to support a credit, trust instruments, proof of state and foreign taxes paid, and appraiser's qualifications should be attached to the return.

## SCHEDULE A: REAL ESTATE

List real property owned only by the decedent. List jointly owned real property on Schedule E. Check local law to determine what is real property and what is a fixture, or personal property. Cemetery lots for the family are excluded. Real property used in a trade or business is reported on Schedule F, Other Miscellaneous Property.

> EXAMPLE   John Smith dies owning his home in joint tenancy with right of survivorship with his wife, Kate. The full value of the home is included on Schedule E unless it was acquired by gift, *devise*, bequest, or inheritance.

Include the full value of all real property, land, and improvements owned outright (free of debt) or indicate if the decedent was personally liable for any mortgages or debts on the property. The amount of the mortgage or debt is then listed on Schedule K, Debts of Decedent, and Mortgages and Liens.

> EXAMPLE   John Smith dies owning vacant land in Chicago with a fair market value of $80,000. The unpaid portion of the loan taken to buy the property is $45,000. Mr. Smith was personally liable for the note. The amount included on Schedule A will be $80,000 with the loan of $45,000 included on Schedule K.

Include the net value of real property (but not less than 0) if the decedent was not personally liable for any mortgages or debts on the property (without recourse).

EXAMPLE    John Smith dies owning a home in Chicago with a fair market value of $100,000 and a mortgage on the property of $45,000. If the mortgage is not paid and the bank's only option is to foreclose on the home (non-recourse), the amount included on Schedule A will be $55,000 ($100,000 less $45,000).

Include the full value of any real property decedent contracted to purchase. The unpaid amount is listed in Schedule K.

EXAMPLE    John Smith dies after contracting to buy a home in Chicago with a purchase price of $175,000. He had given the builder a down payment of $10,000. The home is almost finished. Include on Schedule A the fair market value of the home, $175,000, and include on Schedule K the unpaid liability of $165,000.

Enter a complete description of the property on Schedule A to include the street address. The Taxpayer Relief Act of 1997 added a new provision for conservation easements. Internal Revenue Code §2031(c) allows an executor to make an election to reduce the value of real property included in the decedent's estate for qualifying conservation easements. A conservation easement is a contribution of an interest in qualified real property to a charitable organization exclusively for conservation purposes. This is an exclusion based on the lesser of an applicable percentage amount or a graduated rate, which starts at $100,000 in 1998 and increases to $500,000 in future years. The election, once made, is irrevocable. There are numerous requirements to include reductions for debt-financed property and the value of any development rights retained by the donor.

## SCHEDULE B: STOCKS AND BONDS

List stocks and bonds owned solely by the decedent at the date of death. Also, include stocks and bonds held as a tenant in common in a community property state. List jointly owned stocks and bonds on Schedule E. If the estate paid any foreign estate taxes on stocks or bonds, group these items together and write "Subject to Foreign Death Taxes" on the schedule.

List stocks and bonds together with any declared but unpaid dividends at their fair market value at date of death or alternate valuation date if used. If a dividend is declared prior to decedent's death but payable to stockholders of record on a date that is after the decedent's death, the dividends are not included in the gross estate for estate-tax purposes. To determine the fair market value of a stock or bond, compute the mean between the highest and lowest selling price quoted on the valuation date. If there were no sales of the stock on the valuation date, you must find the fair market value by prorating sales from the nearest trading days before and after the valuation date. If there were no sales of bonds on the valuation date, see Treasury Regulation §20.2031-2(b).

These instructions provide the following method for prorating the closing prices of stock:

- Find the mean between the highest and lowest selling prices on nearest trading dates before and after the valuation date
- Prorate the difference between the two figures to the valuation date
- Add or subtract this prorated difference to the mean price figured for the date nearest the valuation date

EXAMPLE    Mr. Smith died January 15, 1996, owning five hundred shares of ABC Corporation stock not listed on any exchange. On January 15, the shares were being sold at $75 per share. On July 15 (the alternate valuation date six months after date of death), no shares of ABC were sold, but since the market had fallen and the shares had decreased in value, the executor elects the alternate valuation date. The nearest trading dates before and after July 15 were July 13, when the price was $50 per share, and July 16, when the price was $42 per share. The fair market value of the stock is determined as follows:

## STEP 1

Find the mean price for nearest trading days before and after the valuation date. On July 13, one hundred shares of ABC were sold at $51 per share, and thirty shares were sold at $48 per share. The mean price on July 13 is:

$$100 \times \$51 = \$5,100$$
$$30 \times \$48 = \$1,440$$
$$\$6,540 \div 130 = \$50.31$$

On July 16, seventy-five shares of ABC were sold at $44 per share, and twenty shares were sold at $39 per share. The mean price on July 16 is:

$$75 \times \$44 = \$3,300$$
$$20 \times \$39 = \$780$$
$$\$4,080 \div 95 = \$42.95$$

## STEP 2

Prorate the difference between the mean prices to the valuation date.

| July 13 | $50.31 |
|---------|--------|
| July 16 | $42.95 |
| 3 days | $ 7.36 (decreasing in value) |

$$\$7.36 \div 3 \text{ days} = \$2.45 \text{ per day}$$

## STEP 3

Add or subtract the difference in Step 2 to the mean value on the nearest trading date to the alternate valuation date of July 15.

| Nearest trading date | July 16 |
|----------------------|---------|
| Mean value | $42.95 |
| Difference | 2.45 |
| Fair Market Value of ABC on July 15 | $45.40 |

The value of ABC Corporation stock would be listed at $45.40 per share on Schedule B. If ABC Corporation had declared stock dividends on November 21, 1995, to stockholders of record on January 12, 1996 (Mr. Smith died January 15, 1996), which had not been paid by the date of death, the value of the dividends would be listed on Schedule B under the ABC Corporation stock. Include a complete description of stocks and bonds on Schedule B as follows:

| STOCKS | BONDS |
|--------|-------|
| Number of shares | Quantity and denomination |
| Common or preferred | Name of obligor |
| Exact name of corporation | Maturity date |
| Principal exchange traded | |
|    (NYSE, NASDAQ, etc.) | Interest rate |
| *CUSIP* number | Interest due date |
| | Principal exchange listed |
| | CUSIP number |

If the stock or bond is not listed on an exchange, include the company's principal business address. The Committee on Uniform Security Identification Procedure (CUSIP) number can be obtained from either the shares or transfer agent.

Revenue Ruling 59-60, 1959-1 C.B. 237, provides factors that should be considered in valuing the stock of closely held companies where a ready market for the stock does not exist:

- The nature of the business and the history of the enterprise from its inception
- The economic outlook in general and the condition and outlook of the specific industry in particular
- The book value of the stock and the financial condition of the business
- The earning capacity of the company
- The dividend-paying capacity
- Whether or not the enterprise has goodwill or other intangible value
- Sales of the stock and the size of the block of stock to be sold
- The market price of stocks of corporations engaged in the same or a similar line of business that have their stocks actively traded in a free and open market, either on an exchange or over-the-counter

Section 303 of the Internal Revenue Code provides that if the value of closely held corporate stock exceeds 35 percent of the adjusted gross value of the estate, the corporation can buy the shares from the estate, and the transaction will be considered a purchase and sale. Dividends will not be imputed to the estate. In order to qualify, the amount of the purchase price cannot exceed the total estate taxes payable and the amount of funeral and administration expenses allowable as deductions for the estate.

## SCHEDULE C: MORTGAGES, NOTES, AND CASH

List mortgages and notes payable to the decedent alone. If jointly owned, they are reported on Schedule E. Mortgages and notes payable by the decedent are included, if at all, on Schedule K. Group the items in the following order:

- *Mortgages.* Include the face value of the mortgage, date of maturity, name of holder of the mortgage, property secured by the mortgage, interest dates, and rate of interest.

- *Promissory notes.* Include in the same manner as mortgages.
- *Contract to sell land.* Include buyer's name, contract date, property description, contract price, down payment, amount of installment payments, balance due contract, and interest rate.
- *Cash on hand.* List cash not held in an account.
- *Cash in banks, savings and loans, and other financial institutions.* List the name and address of each institution, amount in each account, serial numbers if applicable, type of account, i.e., checking, saving, certificate of deposit.

When reviewing the decedent's accounts, distinguish between gifts to the decedent and payment of loans. Include accrued interest in the valuation.

## SCHEDULE D: INSURANCE ON THE DECEDENT'S LIFE

List insurance on the decedent's life even if the proceeds are not included in the gross estate. If the proceeds are not included, attach an explanation as to why part or all of the proceeds are not included. Request Form 712— Life Insurance Statement—from each insurance company and attach to the back of Schedule D. Include insurance policies if the proceeds are used to pay expenses of the estate, unless the spouse is named the beneficiary of the policy. If the policy is owned by the spouse, the proceeds will qualify for the marital deduction. Include on Schedule D net proceeds received from the following:

- Insurance on the decedent's life receivable by or for the benefit of the estate. If the decedent owned a policy payable to himself, or if there is an obligation for the beneficiary of the policy to use the proceeds for the benefit of the estate, such as to pay taxes or claims, the proceeds are included in the estate to the extent of the obligation to pay the claims or obligations.
- Insurance on the decedent's life if the decedent had any incidents of ownership. A decedent has incidents of ownership in a policy if the decedent, acting alone or in conjunction with another person:
  (a) Owned the policy
  (b) Had the power to change beneficiaries
  (c) Had the power to surrender or cancel the policy
  (d) Had the power to assign the policy or revoke an *assignment*

(e) Had the power to pledge the policy for a loan
(f) Had the power to obtain from the insurer a loan against the sur-
    render value of the policy
(g) Had a reversionary interest of more than 5 percent of the value of
    the policy immediately prior to death
(h) Had the right to select settlement options on group-term life-
    insurance policies

Include the insurance proceeds if the decedent was obligated to maintain the policy pursuant to a divorce decree for his ex-spouse; the estate is allowed a deduction from the estate to pay the obligation.

- If the decedent transferred ownership of a life insurance policy three years or less prior to his death, the proceeds are included in his estate.
- Do not include proceeds from insurance policies if:
  (a) The only incidents of ownership is to receive dividends from the policy or veto a sale by the trustee if an irrevocable insurance trust
  (b) The policy is a group term life owned by a partnership payable to the partnership
  (c) The decedent transferred all incidents of ownership more than three years prior to his death

## SCHEDULE E: JOINTLY OWNED PROPERTY

In general, the decedent's gross estate includes the full value of property held in joint tenancy less that portion of the value attributable to the consideration furnished or paid by the other joint owner(s). If the decedent's interest and the interest of the other joint owner(s) were acquired by gift, devise, bequest, or inheritance, only the decedent's fractional share of the property is included in his estate.

> EXAMPLE    John and Mary Smith inherit interests in a vacation home in Wisconsin from her parents. They own the vacation home with her two sisters all as joint owners. John dies when the value of the home is $200,000. John's executor should include John's fractional share in the home (¼), or $50,000, on his Form 706, since he acquired his interest by inheritance.

Include on Schedule E property held by the decedent in joint tenancy whether or not the value is includible in the estate. This excludes property held as tenants in common, partnership interests (unless the interest itself is held in joint tenancy), and community property. These property interests would fall under §2033 and will be reported elsewhere on the Form 706. Include in Part 1 the full value of qualified joint interests held by the decedent and spouse unless you can show the spouse previously owned the property and the decedent provided no consideration for his interest.

> EXAMPLE    Mary Jones, a widow, marries John Smith. Mary owns a home from her first marriage. After their marriage, Mary puts John's name on the title for probate avoidance purposes. John paid no consideration to Mary for his interest in the home. The value of the home would not be includible in John's estate.

Include in Part 2 the full value of joint interests not included in Part 1 unless you can show the other owners previously owned the property and the decedent provided no consideration for his interest.

There are three principles involving jointly owned property with regard to estates:

1. *Presumption.* When the decedent owns property in joint tenancy with right of survivorship, the entire value of the property is included in the estate unless it can be shown the surviving joint tenants paid consideration for their interests. The decedent's fractional share is then included in the estate.
2. *Gift/Inheritance.* When the joint owners acquired their interests by gift or inheritance from a third party, the decedent's fractional share is included in the estate.
3. *Spousal.* When the joint owners are only the decedent and spouse, one-half of the value of the property is included in the estate regardless of contribution; but see the example above regarding probate avoidance.

See Treasury Regulation 26 C.F.R. §20.2040-1 for rules on joint interests.

## SCHEDULE F: OTHER MISCELLANEOUS PROPERTY NOT REPORTABLE UNDER ANY OTHER SCHEDULE

Include items that are included in the gross estate of the decedent and not listed on any other schedule. If any one item of artistic or intrinsic value, such as a painting or coin collection, is valued at $3,000 or more, or a collection of similar items is valued greater than $10,000, an appraisal must be attached to the return.

The appraiser's statement (Treasury Regulation 20.2031-6(b)) must be accompanied by a written statement made under penalty of perjury from the executor that the appraisal is complete and describing the independence and qualifications of the appraiser. A list of items that may be included on Schedule F includes the following:

- Debts due the decedent other than those included on Schedule C.
- Business interests with statement of assets and liabilities for five years.
- Insurance on the life of another (attach Form 712).
- §2044 property—Property for which a estate marital deduction was previously allowed and spouse had qualifying income interest for life in the property.
- Claims—tax refunds, lawsuits.
- Rights and royalties.
- Leaseholds.
- Judgments not collected.
- Reversionary or remainder interests.
- Shares of trust funds (attach trust instrument to return).
- Household goods and personal effects.
- Farm products and growing crops.
- Livestock, farm machinery.
- Automobiles, boats, trucks.
- Deferred compensation accounts.
- Partnership interests: If the decedent owned a partnership interest, attach a statement of the assets and liabilities as of the valuation date, and for the previous five years. Also, attach statement of net earnings for the previous five years. Include goodwill in the valuation. Jointly owned partnership interests are listed on Schedule E.

• Real estate owned by the decedent's sole proprietorship. Include on Schedule F rather than Schedule A with same information as required on Schedule A.

If the executor wishes to sell or dispose of household effects prior to an examination of the estate tax return by the IRS, he must send a statement to the local IRS district director under penalties of perjury. The statement must include a list of property and appraisals and qualifications of the appraisers. (See Treasury Regulation 20.2031-6(c).) The executor will be advised by the IRS if an inspection is necessary prior to disposition.

## SCHEDULE G: TRANSFERS DURING DECEDENT'S LIFE

There are five types of transfers made by the decedent that must be reported on Schedule G. You do not have to list transfers if there was a bona fide sale or if no gift-tax return was required to be filed; you do have to list life-insurance policies transferred within three years of death. See Internal Revenue Code §2035(b).

### §2035(C) GIFT TAXES

Gift taxes paid on gifts made within three years of decedent's death by either decedent or decedent's spouse. Attach copies of gift-tax returns filed by decedent's spouse the last three years. If a gift-tax return was not required to be filed, do not include the gift.

### TRANSFERS MADE WITHIN THREE YEARS OF DATE OF DEATH

List the value of any life-insurance policies transferred within three years of date of death. Also, include transfers within three years of date of death of retained life-estate interests (Internal Revenue Code §2036), reversionary interest (§2037), or property subject to a power to revoke (§2038) if the subject property would have been included in the gross estate of decedent but for the transfer.

> EXAMPLE    Father gave his son $10,000 in 1997 and then died in 1999. No gift-tax return was required to be filed, since the $10,000 was under the annual gift-tax exclusion. The $10,000 is not included in Father's gross estate.

> EXAMPLE    Father gave his daughter in 1997 a $25,000 life-insurance policy on his life with a present cash-surrender value of

$10,000. Father died in 1999. Although no gift-tax return was required to be filed in 1997, since the value of the policy, when transferred, was under the annual gift-tax exclusion, the full $25,000 is included in father's estate.

## §2036 TRANSFERS WITH RETAINED LIFE ESTATE

Include the value of any property transferred, unless the transfer was made for full consideration, if the decedent had retained: (a) the right to possession or enjoyment of the property or the right to income from the property; or (b) the right, either alone or with another person, to designate the person or persons who will enjoy the property or income. Include the value of stock transferred that would have been included in the decedent's estate if decedent retained the right to vote the stock of a controlled corporation (either alone or through a related party had a 20 percent or greater interest in a company). Under this section, the decedent must have retained the property or income interests: (a) for his life; (b) for a period not ascertainable without reference to his death; or (c) for any period that does not, in fact, end before his death.

## §2037 TRANSFERS TAKING EFFECT AT DEATH

Include the value of property transferred if the decedent had a 5 percent or greater reversionary interest immediately prior to his death and the transfer of property took effect upon his death. Reversionary interest means the property would have returned to either decedent or his estate, may be subject to power of disposition by him at death, but does not include property if only income would have returned to decedent.

EXAMPLE    A decedent transferred property in trust with income payable to his spouse for life and, upon her death, the remainder to his surviving children and, if there were none, to the decedent or his estate. Since each beneficiary can enjoy the property without surviving the decedent, decedent's reversionary interest is not included in his estate under §2037. If, in fact, the trust corpus had reverted to him, then under §2033 it would be included in his estate. See Treasury Regulation 20 C.F.R. 20.2037-1.

## §2038 REVOCABLE TRANSFERS

If a decedent, within three years of the date of his death, transferred, released, or relinquished a power to alter, amend, revoke, or terminate an interest in property, the gross estate includes the value of the power. The value will be the full value of the property over which decedent had the power. The value of the transferred property to be included is its fair market value on decedent's death.

> EXAMPLE    If a decedent transferred five hundred shares of stock to his son and died within three years, and the corporation declared a two-for-one stock dividend, the decedent's estate would include the fair market value of the 750 shares on the date of death, assuming that the decedent released a power of appointment over the stock within three years of death.

## SCHEDULE H: POWER OF APPOINTMENT

A power of appointment is the right to determine who will own a piece of property. Include the value of property over which the decedent held a general power of appointment at the date of his death, or the value of property over which the decedent previously held a power of appointment but released such power prior to death if the property would be included in his gross estate by reason of Internal Revenue Code §2035, §2036, or §2037.

In general, the decedent's power of appointment is the authority to exercise a right in favor of the himself, his estate, or his creditors. Powers of appointment not considered in the gross estate include situations where the power is related to the health, education, support, and maintenance of the decedent in accordance with an ascertainable standard, and other minor exceptions.

## SCHEDULE I: ANNUITIES

Include the value of annuities owned by the decedent. Annuities include employer pension plans, individual retirement accounts, Keogh plans, SEP plans, and annuities purchased from financial organizations. Obtain a letter from the plan administrator as to the value of the account on date of death or alternate valuation date. If the administrator sends a Form 712, attach to the back of Schedule I.

## SCHEDULE J: FUNERAL EXPENSES AND EXPENSES INCURRED IN ADMINISTERING PROPERTY SUBJECT TO CLAIMS

The gross estate is allowed deductions for funeral and administrative expenses. Administrative expenses can be claimed on either Schedule J or the estate's Form 1041, but not both. Include the cost of burial, luncheons, and associated expenses for the funeral. For administrative expenses, include fees for executors, appraisals, attorneys, accountants, court costs, and other expenses related to distribution of the estate. State laws determine the allowable administrative expenses of estates. Under Florida law, federal income taxes are not considered administrative expenses of an estate. Therefore, federal income taxes are not deductible under Internal Revenue Code §2053 in Florida.

If the estate is assessed a penalty by the IRS, this is not deductible as an administrative expense; interest may be deducted. Interest on penalties is deductible.

## SCHEDULE K: DEBTS OF THE DECEDENT, AND MORTGAGES AND LIENS

List debts of the decedent that are collectible, and mortgages and liens. Items that should be listed on this schedule are the decedent's loans (but not any nonrecourse loans that are listed on Schedule A as a reduction in the fair market value of the property), federal, state, and local taxes payable, and leases.

Taxes and business expenses accrued but unpaid at the date of death should be included on Schedule K. If a debt or claim is disputed, enter the amount that is not in dispute on the schedule.

## SCHEDULE L: NET LOSSES DURING ADMINISTRATION AND EXPENSES INCURRED IN ADMINISTERING PROPERTY NOT SUBJECT TO CLAIMS

This schedule allows the estate deductions for losses that occurred during administration. Be sure to include relevant information, such as the date of the loss, type, cause, and if reimbursed by insurance. Remember, there is no minimum loss necessary for the deduction for estate purposes as required for federal income taxes.

Unused net operating losses and capital-loss carryovers existing at the termination of the estate are allowed to the beneficiaries who receive the property of the estate. The deductions are allowable on their Form 1040 and in the same character (short-term or long-term) as the estate would have reported. If a corporation succeeds to the property as beneficiary, the losses are reported as short-term capital-loss carryovers.

## SCHEDULE M: BEQUESTS, ETC., TO SURVIVING SPOUSE

List property that passes to the surviving spouse and qualifies for the marital deduction. Only property that is included in the estate qualifies for the deduction. Property that is claimed as a deduction elsewhere on the Form 706 cannot be claimed a second time on Schedule M. *Terminable interests* cannot be claimed unless QTIP property. This includes property included in a QTIP trust if a U.S. citizen, or QDOT if a noncitizen. While property left in a QTIP to the spouse is not taxed in the decedent's estate, it will be included in the spouse's estate, at which time the property may have substantially increased in value.

> EXAMPLE     Husband decides to take advantage of the unlimited marital deduction to defer estate taxes until his spouse dies. Husband's will provides that after the payment of funeral and administrative expenses, all of his property shall be paid to his wife, provided she survive him by thirty days. He also directs his spouse to pay $10,000 to his brother Jack. The $10,000 paid to Jack is not eligible for the unlimited marital deduction.

If the surviving spouse dies prior to the decedent's estate-tax return being filed or is in poor health, calculate the tax due on both estates without claiming the unlimited marital deduction. Due to the graduated rates, it is probably best not to claim the unlimited marital deduction.

---

### CAUTION

If the spouse wishes to disclaim an inheritance, she should do so in writing within nine months of date of death and prior to accepting and treating the property as her own. Even if the spouse, by law, immediately takes title to property, such as upon the death of her husband, she may still disclaim the property within the allotted time frame.

---

## SCHEDULE O: CHARITABLE, PUBLIC, AND SIMILAR GIFTS AND BEQUESTS

List charitable contributions by wills or trusts. See §2055 for guidelines on what property will qualify for a deduction. Property that is disclaimed by a beneficiary to be given to a charity must be disclaimed within nine months of date of death in order to be allowed as a charitable deduction. The charitable deduction rules are different for estate taxes than for income taxes concerning what constitutes a qualifying charity. Under federal income-tax law, charitable contributions are generally limited to qualifying domestic organizations, §170(c). Under estate taxes, charitable deductions are allowed for religious, charitable, scientific, literary, or educational nondomestic organizations, §2055(a)(2). The amount of the deduction is limited to the amount actually transferred to the charity.

## SCHEDULE P: CREDIT FOR FOREIGN DEATH TAXES
In general, you are allowed a credit or deduction for foreign death taxes paid. If the decedent was a citizen or resident of the United States, you may be able to claim a credit for foreign death taxes paid on line 18 of page 1 of Form 706. You must attach Form 706CE, Certificate of Payment of Foreign Death Tax, to support the credit. §2053(d) allows the executor in certain situations to deduct the foreign death taxes from the gross estate on Schedule P. The credit or deduction must be allowed by either statute or treaty. The total credit allowable is limited to the federal estate tax attributable to the property located in the foreign jurisdiction. If death taxes are paid to more than one foreign country, separate computations must be made for each.

## SCHEDULE Q: CREDIT FOR TAX ON PRIOR TRANSFERS
If the decedent received property from someone who died within either two years after or ten years prior to the decedent, a credit for the federal estate tax paid attributable to the property transferred is allowed on line 19 of page 1 of the Form 706. You must complete Schedule Q. While the property received cannot be property with a bare legal ownership, such as when acting as a trustee over the property, it does include less than a complete ownership of properties to comprise life estates, reversionary interests, annuities, and the term for years to the extent the decedent became the beneficial owner of the property. It does not include property over which the decedent received a power of appointment unless it is a general power.

PERCENT OF FEDERAL ESTATE-TAX PAID ALLOWED AS A CREDIT

| | |
|---|---|
| Transferor died not more than 2 years after decedent | 100 |
| Transferor died less than 2 years prior to decedent | 100 |
| Transferor died more than 2 and less than 4 years prior to decedent | 80 |
| Transferor died more than 4 and less than 6 years prior to decedent | 60 |
| Transferor died more than 6 and less than 8 years prior to decedent | 40 |
| Transferor died more than 8 and less than 10 years prior to decedent | 20 |
| Transferor died more than 10 years prior to decedent | 0 |

## SCHEDULE R: GENERATION-SKIPPING TRANSFER TAX

A generation-skipping tax (GST) is imposed on direct skips occurring at death. The law imposes the GST tax on transfers to trusts having beneficiaries more than one generation below the decedent and direct transfers to beneficiaries more than one generation below the decedent. The maximum allowable amount that may be transferred directly to skip persons is $1,000,000 without imposition of the additional tax. The $1,000,000 can be allocated among the transfers by the decedent or his executor. This is an irrevocable election. The current law is effective for transfers after October 22, 1986. If either the decedent was incompetent or the trust was created prior to that date, check with your tax accountant, since the GST may not apply. The GST does not apply for transfers within the $10,000 annual exclusion for gifts or certain payments for tuition and medical expenses.

Generation-skipping transfers include the following three categories:

### TAXABLE TERMINATIONS

Taxable terminations are transfers of an interest in a trust or a portion thereof that occur based upon death, lapse of time, release of power, or otherwise, which result in the interests in the trust being held by generation-skipping beneficiaries. The GST is paid by the trustee.

> EXAMPLE    I transfer property to a trust with the income from the trust to be paid to my son during his lifetime and the corpus of the trust to go to my grandchild upon my son's death. This is not a direct skip since my son is to receive income from the trust. A taxable termination will occur upon my son's death if the property goes to my grandchild. The GST tax is due when my son dies.

### TAXABLE DISTRIBUTIONS

Taxable distributions are transfers from a trust to a skip person. The distribution may be from trust corpus or income. If income, an income-tax deduction is allowed for the GST tax imposed by the recipient. The GST is paid by the skip person.

> EXAMPLE    I transfer property to an irrevocable trust with income to be paid to my son for life and the corpus to be distributed to grandchild upon reaching age twenty-five, with the remainder distributed upon my son's death. The distribution at age twenty-five is a taxable distribution.

### DIRECT SKIPS

A direct skip is a transfer of an interest in property to a skip person. For the purposes of assessing taxes, the IRS defines a skip person as either: (1) a person two or more generations below the decedent; or (2) a trust where all the interests of the trust are held by skip persons, or distributions from the trust can only be made to skip persons. The GST is paid by the trustee.

> EXAMPLE     I have a wife and two sons who are living. One son is married with a daughter. I transfer my vacation home worth $125,000 to my grandchild. Because I have transferred property and passed by my son who is living, this is a direct skip to my grandchild.

### PREDECEASED CHILD EXCLUSION

A transfer is not considered a direct skip if the transfer is made to a grandchild directly because the grandchild's parent is dead at the time of the transfer.

## SCHEDULE S: INCREASED ESTATE TAX ON EXCESS RETIREMENT ACCUMULATIONS

This section was repealed by Taxpayer Relief Act of 1997.

## SCHEDULE T: QUALIFIED FAMILY-OWNED BUSINESS INTEREST DEDUCTION

Section 2057 allows the executor to elect to deduct, with limitations, from the gross value of an estate, the value of a qualified family-owned business interest (QFOB). In order to take a QFOB interest deduction, the following criteria must be met:

- Decedent must have been a citizen or resident of the United States at date of death
- The QFOB interests must be included in the estate-tax return (Form 706)
- The interests must pass to or acquired by a qualified heir
- The adjusted value of the QFOB must exceed 50 percent of the adjusted gross estate
- The business must have its principal place of business in the United States
- The QFOB was owned by decedent or member of decedent's family for five out of the last eight years

- The decedent or member of his family materially participated in the QFOB in five out of the last eight years

To meet the requirements for a QFOB, the business interest must be a sole proprietorship, or interest in an entity carrying on a trade or business, which is:

- At least 50 percent of the entity is owned by decedent or members of decedent's family, or
- At least 70 percent of the entity is owned by members of two families and 30 percent is owned by decedent or members of decedent's family, or
- At least 90 percent of the entity is owned by members of three families and 30 percent is owned by decedent or members of decedent's family

# Gift Taxes

U.S. Gift (and Generation-Skipping Transfer) Tax Return, Form 709, must be filed in many cases when there has been a completed transfer of property. Most times, when a gift-tax return is filed, no tax is due since the person making the gift, the donor, has not used up his unified credit exemption against the tax. Even small estates, which will never pay any estate taxes, could be required to file gift-tax returns. It is the donor who is responsible for filing and paying any tax due on the transfer.

## Points to Consider

- Completed transfers of property for less than full and adequate consideration are generally considered gifts.
- Each person has a $10,000 annual exclusion per person for gifts before a gift-tax return must be filed.
- Gifts of future interests in property do not qualify for the $10,000 annual exclusion.
- No gift-tax return is required for transfers of property between spouses unless the gift was for a terminable interest.
- No gift-tax return is required on donations to charitable organizations unless the transfer was for a partial interest in property.
- Spouses may elect gift-splitting by signing Form 709A, which provides that gifts will be considered to have been made one-half by each even if only one spouse makes the gift.

## Gift-Tax Return Filing Requirements

A gift-tax return must be filed for each calendar year by each person making gifts during the year, except in circumstances listed below. A gift-tax return is required on transfers for less than adequate consideration unless:

- The spouse receiving the gift is a U.S. citizen and the gift is not a terminable interest
- The spouse receiving the gift was not a U.S. citizen, but the spouse received $100,000 or less; and the gift was not a terminable interest
- No person receiving a gift received more than $10,000
- No partial interests were given to charities
- No gift was for a future interest in property

## Gift-Tax Return Filing Date

A gift-tax return is due by April 15 after the end of the year in which reportable gifts are made. If an individual receives an extension of time to file his income-tax return, the time for filing the gift-tax return is also extended to that date. If a reportable gift is made during the year the donor dies, the time for filing the gift-tax return is the time for filing the estate-tax return (Form 706), unless the time for filing the Form 706 is later than April 15 of the following year, in which case the gift-tax return is due April 15. Applications for extending the filing date for the gift-tax return must contain a full explanation of the reasons for the extension request. Except for donors who are overseas, extensions will not be granted for more than six months. An extension of the filing date does not extend the date for paying the tax. An extension of time to pay the tax may be granted upon a showing of undue hardship. This must be more than an inconvenience to the taxpayer; it must be shown that the taxpayer may suffer a substantial financial loss.

## Exclusions from the Gift Tax

In order to qualify for the annual $10,000 per-person exclusion, the property interest transferred must be for a present interest. One important exception is a transfer to a minor's trust per Internal Revenue Code §2503(c). This section provides that gifts to minors less than twenty-one years of age are not considered gifts of future interests if the property and income therefrom: (1) may be expended by or for the benefit of the minor before reaching age twenty-one; and (2) if not spent, will pass to the minor when he reaches age twenty-one, and if the minor dies before reaching age twenty-one, the trust will be payable to the minor's estate or whomever he selects under a power of appointment.

Transfers for certain educational or medical expenses are also excluded from taxable gifts. The gift tax is not imposed on services rendered that you provide to someone for free. The gift tax applies to a transfer by way of gift regardless if the transfer was in trust, direct or indirect, whether the property is real or personal, tangible or intangible. Taxable transfers may be created by transfers to trusts, forgiveness of indebtedness, assignment of judgments, assignment of benefits of an insurance policy, transfers of cash or certificates of deposit.

The transfer of property or interests in property pursuant to a written agreement between spouses in a divorce is considered a transfer for full and adequate consideration and not a gift. The spouses must obtain a final decree of divorce within two years after entering into a written agreement. Also, transfers to provide reasonable support for children are not considered gifts.

A person who makes a qualified disclaimer of property is not considered to have made a gift, because the property is considered to pass directly from the donor to the next beneficiary.

Although charitable gifts from a decedent's estate are allowed as a deduction on the estate-tax return, no income-tax charitable deduction is allowed on the decedent's final income-tax return. Gifts to charitable organizations during one's lifetime can be deducted up to certain limits on the income-tax return.

## Present, Terminable, and Future Interests in Property

In order to qualify for the annual $10,000 exclusion, the property interest transferred must be for a present interest. A present interest in property is an unrestricted right to the immediate use, possession, or enjoyment of property or the income from the property, such as a life estate.

A terminable interest in property is one that ends at a certain time or when a contingency occurs or fails to occur. Examples include estates for a term period, life estates, and annuities. Joint tenancies and tenancies by the entirety between spouses are not considered terminable interests.

Future interests in property include *reversions,* remainders, and other interests, whether vested or contingent, which are limited to commence in use and possession at some future date. This does not include contractual rights, such as exist in bonds, notes, or life-insurance policies.

Examples of transfers of interests included in the regulations (26 C.F.R §25.2503-3(c)) include the following:

A creates a trust for the benefit of B. The trustee is directed to pay the net income of the trust to B for as long as B shall live. The trustee also has the power to withhold payment in any year if the trustee deems this best and add the income to the principal of the trust. B does not have a present interest in the trust since the trustee can withhold the payments. Transfers to the trust do not qualify for the $10,000 exclusion.

C transfers life-insurance policies on his life to a trust for the benefit of D. Upon C's death, the proceeds are to be invested with the income payable to D for his lifetime. Since the income payments will not begin until after C's death, the transfer of life-insurance policies to the trust is a gift of a future interest.

E creates a trust for the benefit of his three children and transfers cash to the trust. Although the trustee must distribute all of the net income of the trust each year to the children, he can use his own discretion as to which child shall receive how much money. This is not a gift of a present interest and transfers to the trust do not qualify for the $10,000 exclusion.

F pays premiums on a life insurance policy on his life. G owns the policy. The payments of the premiums are gifts of present interests qualifying for the $10,000 exclusion.

## Tax Basis of Gifts

The tax basis of a gift is the lower of the fair market value on the date of the gift or the donor's basis, plus any gift taxes paid on the transfer. Inherited assets receive a stepped-up basis to fair market value on the date of death or alternate valuation date six months later if so elected. This is why if you have purchased stock that has decreased in value, instead of making a gift of the stock, you should sell the stock, claim the capital loss on your income-tax return, and gift the proceeds. The recipient can always use the cash to buy the same stock.

## Stock Options

Many large companies are now using stock options to retain a highly qualified work force. A transfer of a nonstatutory stock option for no consideration from a father who has been awarded the options at work to his
child is considered a completed gift on the later of either the transfer or
the time when the child's interest to exercise the option to buy the stock is
no longer subject to any conditions prior to being executed. If options
have been granted to the father and can be exercised after three years of
working, when the three years have passed and the child can exercise the
option, a completed gift has been made.

# 12

# Marital Status, Health, and Your Estate

This chapter contains several issues that are important to estate planning. Your marital status can affect not only the future distribution of wealth to your heirs, but also your own financial expectations. And, while no one likes to think about losing his health or competency, investigating caretaking and assisted-living options now could save you and your relatives money, time, and frustration in the future.

## Marriage and Divorce

Except for Hollywood stars and wealthy individuals, most people tend to ignore the financial impact of marriages and divorces. Some of the wealthy persons draw up prenuptial agreements in cases of divorces to decide the finances after the separation. Most of us, however, think very little of finances or estate planning while getting married or divorced.

There are many financial ramifications when a couple decides either to join together or to split apart. It is not uncommon for individuals who have lost their partners of many years to remarry and enjoy life to its fullest extent. It is also a fact that a high percentage of marriages end in divorce. Estate planning when a marriage or divorce is contemplated is important for ensuring inheritance for children from previous marriages, providing security for the second spouse, dealing with numerous tax issues, and making sure there is money left for health-care costs. If either a marriage or divorce is part of your future, you should contact your local bar association for a list of attorneys who are experts in both the estate-planning and tax aspects of marriages and divorces.

## MARRIAGE

If you have children from a first marriage and have a clause in your will that leaves everything to your current spouse, then your own children could possibly receive nothing when you die, since all of your property will go to your new spouse. If these children are grown (age eighteen), they do not have a statutory right to inherit your property. A safe method is to execute new wills and trusts with a qualified terminal-interest property trust (QTIP). This will provide income for your current spouse and leave your property to your children.

- Upon remarriage (or divorce), draft new wills, powers of attorney for property, and health-care directives.
- Change designations on bank signature cards, IRA accounts, 401(k) plans, insurance policies, investment accounts, safe-deposit boxes.
- If you are receiving a widow(er) pension, check with the plan administrator to make sure remarrying will not void the pension benefits.
- Make sure each spouse has a property titled in his own name to take advantage of the unified credit amount.
- If you owned the residence prior to the marriage and after the marriage place your spouse's name on the title, make sure there are accurate records to reflect that you owned the property outright prior to marriage, for estate-tax purposes.
- Consider entering into a prenuptial agreement. While it may not be enforceable in court at a later date, the inventory will provide additional evidence of ownership of property for estate-tax purposes.

## DIVORCE

A divorce occurring after the execution of a will treats the ex-spouse as though he or she had died (Illinois). The ex-spouse does not receive any legacies, interests, powers of appointment, or nomination as executor or trustee. Generally, alimony is includible as taxable income by the recipient and deductible by the payor. The payments must be required by the divorce decree and not voluntary. The parties can reach an agreement that the payments are not taxable or deductible. There are recapture provisions to watch for if the amount of the payments change or terminate.

Transfers of property between the spouses pursuant to a divorce decree are not taxable. The recipient inherits the cost basis, not fair market value. Watch for liabilities in excess of basis, however, which could trigger taxable income. When dividing property, consider the future tax consequences. If the husband receives stock A with a fair market value of $150,000 and a cost basis of $145,000, while the wife receives stock B with the same fair market value but a cost basis of $50,000, the wife will end up paying considerably more in income taxes when the stock is sold.

Generally, the custodial parent can claim the personal tax exemptions for the children. The spouses can agree to let the noncustodial parent claim the tax exemptions. Since personal exemptions are phased out after adjusted gross income reaches a certain amount, it may not be advantageous for the high-income earner to request the exemptions.

A Qualified Domestic Relations Order, Internal Revenue Code §414(p), provides that a spouse can share in the other spouse's qualified retirement plan benefits. A state court order for child support, alimony, or transfer of property that results in payments from a retirement plan (which can start even before the working spouse retires), will not be subject to the 10 percent penalty for early withdrawal, Internal Revenue Code §72(t). The payments will not be taken into consideration of the 15 percent penalty on excess distributions from retirement plans, and the payments can be rolled over into an IRA.

If your ex-spouse requests that you sign an income-tax return so you can file a joint income-tax return for the prior year (if you were married on the last day of the year), use caution if you suspect all income is not reported or there are doubtful deductions. If you sign the joint return and it is audited by the IRS, you can be held liable for any additional taxes, interest, and penalties individually. The IRS can go after either party that signs the return. There are innocent-spouse provisions, but only if you meet the set criteria. Consider filing with a status of Married Filing Separate if you have any doubts.

## TAX ISSUES INCIDENT TO A DIVORCE
- When transferring a closely held business (stock) to a family member, consider placing the shares in a trust rather than an outright transfer to an individual. Make sure the trust has a right of first refusal to buy the shares in case a court decides to transfer the shares to the divorcing spouse.

> ## CAUTION
>
> Specificity is needed in divorce decrees in providing an ex-spouse survivor benefits. An appeals-court case found, federal retirement law states that a former spouse is not eligible for a survivor annuity unless it is expressly provided for, and that a divorce decree must either state the former spouse's entitlement to a survivor annuity or direct the federal employee or retiree to provide a former spouse with an annuity.

- Consider the use of an alimony trust under Internal Revenue Code §682 if the spouse is careless with money (gambler, heavy drinker).
- There are numerous tax considerations when couples get divorced. Issues include alimony vs. child support, alimony recapture, transfers of property, which party is entitled to claim exemptions for children, deductibility of legal fees, etc.
- Transfer of income-producing property, such as U.S. savings bonds, may result in taxable income.
- The transfer of an individual retirement account pursuant to a divorce decree does not result in a taxable transaction. Internal Revenue Code §408(d)(6).
- Be careful of (in excess of $10,000) split-interest gifts prior to divorce, which use up the unified credit.
- Generally, legal fees for the divorce are not deductible. To be deductible, legal fees have to be related to the production of income or tax advice.
- When negotiating a divorce settlement, make sure there is a provision to share any documents needed for tax purposes.

It is possible that couples in the near future may find it advantageous to file for divorce and transfer property pursuant to a divorce decree. For example, if a spouse suddenly needs long-term medical care, they may file for divorce and obtain a court decree transferring assets. This would avoid the Medicaid-prohibited transfers within thirty-six months, since the transfer would be pursuant to the court order. There also may be estate-tax advantages for divorces of wealthier couples. Hopefully, couples will not file for divorce just for the above reasons—money isn't everything.

## Nursing Homes

An extremely difficult and sensitive topic for many people is the issue of nursing homes. However, there often comes a time when, for medical and safety considerations, placement in a nursing home is the only viable alternative for the care of a parent or other relative. There are many different considerations in choosing a retirement (nursing) home. There are various levels of care available, some will take Medicaid patients and some will not, some treat this strictly as a business and some do this for charitable considerations. Most homes have long waiting lists for placement. If a nursing home is possible in the future, do not wait until the last minute assuming a person will be admitted. Start your search early. Make appointments and visit various homes, obtain financial requirements and review applications.

Some nursing homes are considered skilled nursing facilities, which provide posthospital care for patients who are discharged from the hospital but cannot return home without twenty-four-hour supervision. These facilities are allowed to charge higher fees than normally allowed by Medicare because they handle patients requiring complex and costly care. The number of skilled nursing facilities granted exemption to charge higher fees has grown from 80, during fiscal years 1979–92, to 552 in 1995, according to a government report.[1]

There are approximately 1,200 continuing-care retirement communities that provide managed services for 350,000 residents.[2] These communities provide proactive methods to improve the health and prolong the lives of its residents. They encourage exercise, proper nutrition, social activities, immunizations, and health exams. Most of these communities are nonprofit organizations with religious affiliations. Across the country, dementia and Alzheimer disease are increasing in frequency, since the population is living longer. This results in a very difficult, if not impossible, situation when you are trying simultaneously to raise children and to provide the necessary care needed for an afflicted adult.

Take the time to visit the homes well in advance. Find out their requirements for admission, security, staffing levels, ownership, visiting

---

[1]Government Accounting Office/Health and Human Services Audit Report 97-18, December 1996.
[2]Government Accounting Office/Health and Human Services Audit Report 97-36, January 1997.

hours, medical services provided, resident activities, number of residents, and levels of care offered.

Some nursing homes have units similar to single-family homes, which can be "purchased" with a refundable deposit. The advantages include staff checking on a person daily, twenty-four-hour medical attention, and the availability of meals and activities. Also, the resident can be transferred to a higher level of care within the nursing home when necessary, without a long waiting list. If this is a potential option, place your name on the waiting list as soon as possible.

---

### CAUTION

Refundable deposits on nursing home units, which can cost well in excess of $100,000, are currently not subject to any government guarantee similar to the deposits in a bank with the FDIC. A large nursing facility recently went bankrupt, and the customers who had deposited large amounts of money are out of luck. Check the financial statements of the nursing facility if you are depositing large sums of money. Ask if the money is held in a trust or being spent on current maintenance.

---

Starting in 1997, nursing-home costs could be deductible as a medical deduction on tax returns. Since nursing-home costs can be $5,000 or more per month, check with your tax accountant to see if you are eligible. If you make improvements in your home for medical reasons, such as a special bath to treat your arthritis, check with your tax accountant on its deductibility as a medical expense. Always have a doctor put it in writing as evidence for any IRS audit.

## LEGAL RIGHTS OF NURSING-HOME RESIDENTS

Residents of nursing homes have the same rights as any U.S. citizen. The Illinois Nursing Home Care Act, 210 ILCS 45/1-10 et. seq., covers rights of residents, responsibilities of the home, and related matters. If you believe a nursing home has violated the rights of someone, you may consider contacting an attorney to pursue the issue. The attorney may be awarded attorney fees if your side prevails in the lawsuit. A resident's settlement proceeds of a lawsuit against a nursing home for injuries sustained is not subject to the Illinois Department of Public Aid lien.

Under federal law, 42 U.S.C. §3000 et. seq., states are required to establish ombudsman programs to assist nursing-home residents with resolving complaints and grievances regarding their care. Grievances that are not resolved at the local level may then be referred to the Department of Health in Illinois. The federal government funds the programs. The ombudsman visits nursing homes, provides information, and holds conferences regarding long-term care. He also advocates for legislation to improve conditions when allowed by law. The Illinois program is under the Illinois Department of Aging.

# Glossary

**A Trust:** Common name for a marital trust prior to the unlimited marital deduction.

**Abatement:** Decrease in the amount of a gift or *legacy* due to insufficiency of estate property.

**Ademption:** Cancellation of a gift or legacy due to an act of the testator, as when testator sells the particular item.

**Adverse Possession:** Acquiring title to real property through actual, open, notorious, exclusive, and without permission, use of the property for a certain time period established by law.

**Administrator:** Person selected by a court to manage a decedent's estate when there is no executor named in a will or capable of taking the office.

**Affidavit of Heirship:** A written statement listing the heirs of a decedent, signed and certified to.

**Alternate Valuation Date:** Internal Revenue Code §2032 allows the executor to elect to value the gross estate at its fair market value six months from the date of death.

**Anatomical Gift:** Gift of vital organs.

**Ancillary Probate:** Process of conducting probate in a state other than where the decedent was *domiciled* due to property located in the other state.

**Annual Exclusion:** The amount ($10,000 per year) a donor can give to any number of persons without filing a gift-tax return or paying federal estate taxes.

**Annuity:** A series of payments made at regular intervals. The buyer of the annuity pays a set amount and selects a payout method. Payouts may be monthly, quarterly, annually, lump-sum, for life, for a term certain, or joint life and survivor.

**Annuitant:** Individual receiving benefits from an annuity.

**Assignment:** An arrangement between a doctor or medical equipment provider and Medicare whereby the doctor or provider agrees to accept the Medicare-approved amount for services and supplies under Part B. Medicare generally pays 80 percent after the patient has met the deductible of $100, with the patient paying 20 percent.

**Attestation Clause:** Statement following the testator's signature signed by the witnesses to the will that they witnessed the testator sign the will in their presence and that the testator appeared of sound mind and under no duress.

**Beneficiary:** Person receiving property from an estate, or named in a trust agreement.

**Beneficiary Designation Forms:** Forms provided by insurance companies and financial institutions for the owner of an account to select who will receive the account upon the owner's death.

**Benefit Period:** The period in which benefits will be covered by Medicare. A benefit period begins the day the patient is hospitalized and ends when the patient has been out of the facility for sixty consecutive days.

**Bequest:** Gift of personal property by will; see **devise** (land).

**Bypass Trust:** An estate-planning technique that takes advantage of each spouse's unified credit. If property is titled correctly (in each spouse's name alone), and each spouse's will or trust includes a bypass trust, this method can shelter $1,200,000 (1998) of property from federal estate taxes. If one spouse has significantly more in assets than the other, the technique will work only if the wealthier spouse dies first.

**Capacity:** Legal ability to execute a valid will, trust, power of attorney, or contract. The individual must be eighteen years of age, of sound mind, and not under any undue influence or other legal impediment (Illinois).

**Charitable Lead Trust:** An irrevocable trust established by a grantor with the trust income donated to a qualifying charity for a term of years with the grantor or others receiving the remainder interest.

**Charitable Lead Annuity Trust:** A charitable lead trust whereby the annual payout is equal to a fixed percentage of the net assets at the inception of the trust.

**Charitable Lead Unitrust:** A charitable lead trust whereby the annual payout is a fixed percentage of the net assets of the trust at the end of each year.

**Charitable Trust:** An irrevocable trust created by a grantor for the benefit of a charity, which generally provides the grantor with a charitable income tax deduction. There are various options that can be selected in drafting the trust. Both charitable organizations and private individuals can be named beneficiaries.

**[Charitable Remainder Annuity Trust (CRAT)]**

**Charitable Remainder Trust:** Irrevocable transfer of a remainder interest in income-producing property to a trust with the trustor (or beneficiaries designated by the trustor) retaining a life interest in the income. A CRT provides a current charitable income-tax deduction for the present value of the remainder interest. The payment to the trustor (or beneficiaries) can be a fixed amount (unitrust) or a fixed percentage of the value of the trust property (annuity trust).

**[Charitable Remainder Unitrust (CRUT)]**

**Claim:** For probate purposes, any cause of action filed within the statutory-claim period.

**Clifford Trust:** Type of trust previously used to shift income taxes from a grantor to another for a ten-year period at which time the trust principal and income would revert to the grantor. No longer in use due to changes in tax law.

**Closely Held Company:** A company, the ownership of which is held by one or a small number of individuals.

**Codicil:** Change or amendment to a will; generally used for minor changes in the will.

**Coinsurance:** The portion a Medicare-approved patient must pay.

**Community Property:** Property (with exceptions) acquired by a couple during the time they live together or are married, which is treated as owned by both parties.

**Conservator:** Person selected by a court to manage the financial affairs of an incompetent adult.

**Corporate Successor Trustee:** A legal entity authorized to act in a fiduciary capacity in the state.

**Credit-Shelter Trust:** A trust established to accept the amount of property excluded from the federal estate tax by the unified credit exclusion.

**Creditor-Protection Laws:** Statutes designed to protect debtors from their creditors.

***Crummey* Powers Trust:** A procedure for creating a present interest in the beneficiaries of a trust for transfers of cash to a life-insurance trust, which is used for the payment of insurance premiums. Without a present interest, the transfers cannot be considered excludable gifts. In PLR 9030005, the IRS said a thirty-day withdrawal right was sufficient. The name came from a court case, *Crummey v. Commissioner,* 397 F2d (9th circuit, 1968). There are also Hanging *Crummey* Powers written into trust agreements.

**Curtesy:** Common-law term for the right of a widower to an interest in real property his wife owned.

**CUSIP:** Acronym for Committee on Uniform Security and Identification Procedure. A nine-digit number assigned for traded securities.

**Custodian Accounts:** Financial accounts in the care of a person or corporation with a duty to preserve and protect the property.

**[Decedent]**

**Demise:** Pass by will or inheritance; also death.

**Devastavit:** The failure or refusal of an estate representative to pay money or deliver property to person entitled pursuant to a lawful order of court, which may lead to action upon the representative's bond.

**Descendant:** Person directly related, such as child, grandchild.

**Devise:** A gift of real property (land and things affixed to land) by a will.

**Disclaimer:** Process often used in postmortem estate planning whereby an individual informs the administrator of an estate that he does not wish to receive certain property. In order to be valid, the disclaimer must be in writing prior to receiving the property, must identify the property, and be executed within nine months of date of death.

**Discretionary Trust:** A trust that allows the trustees to distribute or accumulate trust income and principal as they deem best in their own judgment.

**Distributable Net:** The taxable income of an estate or trust. See Internal Revenue Income Code §643.

**Domicile:** A person's legal home.

**Donee:** Person receiving a gift.

**Donor:** Person making a gift.

**Dower:** Common-law term for the right of a widow to an interest in real property her husband owned.

**Dynasty Trust:** A name given to a generation-skipping-transfer trust that may hold funds for an extended period of time. Several states, such as Delaware and Alaska, have enacted laws permitting such trusts. These type of trusts are generally used by only the very wealthy.

**Easements:** A right to use the land of another for a special purpose.

**Educational Individual Retirement Account:** A tax-deferred account allowed under Internal Revenue Code §530 for the purpose of paying qualified higher education expenses of a beneficiary.

**Electing Small Business Trust:** An ESBT, under §1361 of the Internal Revenue Code, may be a shareholder in a Subchapter S corporation pursuant to the Taxpayer Relief Act of 1997.

**Equitable Title:** The ownership interest of a person in property that is held by another with legal title, for example, the beneficiary of a trust.

**Escheat:** Procedure whereby a decedent's property passes to the state when no valid heir or beneficiary can be located.

**Estate:** Total of all real and personal property owned or controlled by a decedent at the time of his death and any future increases or decreases until distribution thereof.

**Exclusion Amount:** The amount of property not subject to federal estate taxation by the unified credit.

**Execute:** Completing the necessary steps to make a legal document valid or transaction complete. Some documents are executed with a signature alone while others must be signed, witnessed, and notarized. There must be an actual delivery of property for a valid gift for tax purposes.

**Executor:** Person or corporation named in a will to administer a decedent's estate. Called Executrix, if female.

**Fair Market Value:** The price that a willing buyer would pay to a seller, both with full knowledge of the facts and neither being under any compulsion to buy or sell.

**Family Partnership:** A tax-planning technique whereby parents transfer property into partnership with their children designated as limited partners. Transfers of interest in the partnership can be excluded by the annual gift exclusion, and valuation of property may be less, due to minority discounts.

**Fee Simple Absolute:** 100 percent ownership of property.

**Fiduciary:** A person in a position of trust and confidence, with duties and responsibilities over the subject matter.

**Future Interest:** An interest or right in property that may occur at some future time; includes reversions and remainders.

[**Generation-Skipping Tax**]

**Generation-Skipping-Transfer Tax Exemption:** Internal Revenue Code §2631(a) allows each person to transfer up to $1,000,000 in property to a person two generations below without subjecting property to the generation-skipping tax.

**Generation-Skipping Trust (GST):** A trust established to hold property for which the transferor made the GST exemption.

**Gift:** A transfer of property made without consideration by a donor having the requisite capacity (age, absence of duress, and mental capability) to a donee who accepts the property. To constitute a valid gift for tax-law purposes, the gift must have actually been delivered, not a promise of a future gift.

**Gift Tax:** Internal Revenue Code §2501 imposes a tax on the transfer of property by gift. The first $10,000 of each gift to a different individual may be excluded (other than gifts of future interests in property).

**Gifts *Causa Mortis:*** Gifts made in contemplation of death. Such gifts may or may not be valid, depending on state law. There are issues regarding whether this was an actual gift, or promise to make a future gift followed by lack of delivery of the gift.

**Grantor:** Person who transfers property into a trust.

**Grantor-Retained Annuity Trust:** An irrevocable trust to which a person, the grantor, transfers property and retains an income interest in the property during the term of the trust, with designated beneficiaries receiving the trust property at the end of the trust term. The trust pays the grantor a fixed annuity amount for the duration of the trust. The value of the gift to the beneficiaries is determined as the value of the initial transfer of property less the value of grantor's retained interest. There can be only the initial funding of the trust; later additions by the grantor are not allowed.

**Grantor-Retained Income Trust:** An irrevocable trust that pays the grantor all of the trust income earned each year. This trust is seldom used anymore.

**Grantor Retained Unitrust:** An irrevocable trust that pays the grantor a fixed percentage of the net trust assets each year. The trust must be appraised each year, and there can only be the initial funding of the trust. Later additions to the trust property by the grantor are not allowed.

**[Grantor Trust]**

**Guardian:** Person appointed by a court to represent interests of minors and adults under a legal disability.

**Health-Care Power of Attorney:** A medical directive allowed by state law, which authorizes a designated agent certain rights concerning the health care of the principal.

**Heir:** Person who inherits based on a blood relationship.

**Holographic Will:** A will in the handwriting of a person that is not witnessed; not recognized as valid in many states.

**Homestead Exemption:** An amount allowed as a reduction in real property taxes on the primary residence of a taxpayer.

**Hospice:** Health-care service for the terminally ill.

**Independent Administration:** Conducting the administration of a decedent's estate with minimal court supervision; relatively simple and inexpensive procedure, as opposed to supervised administration.

**Income in Respect of a Decedent (IRD):** Items subject to income taxes that were not taxed during a decedent's lifetime.

**Individual Retirement Account (IRA):** An account placed in trust allowed by §408 of the Internal Revenue Code, which allows the account to grow tax-free until a future date.

**Intervivos:** During a person's lifetime.

**Intestate:** Dying without leaving a valid will.

**Irrevocable Life-Insurance Trust:** A trust established to hold life-insurance policies that will keep the proceeds of the policies out of the taxable estate of the decedent.

**IRS Levy:** An assessment of tax by the IRS.

**Joint Tenancy:** Form of ownership where property is owned by two or more individuals who each have an undivided interest in the whole property.

**Land Trust:** A means of holding title to real estate where the trustee is generally a bank.

**Lapse:** A gift or legacy that fails during the donor's lifetime.

**Legacy:** A testamentary disposition of real or personal property and includes devise and bequest.

**Legal Title:** Actual evidence of ownership of property as opposed to equitable ownership. A trustee is said to have legal title while the beneficiaries have equitable title.

**Letters of Office, or Letter Testamentary:** Authority issued by a court granting an executor or administrator power to settle an estate.

**Life Estate:** The right to use property or receive income until death.

**Limited Guardianship:** A person with authority and responsibility to manage either the financial affairs or care of either a minor or a person under a disability.

**Limiting for Charge:** The maximum amount a doctor may charge a Medicare patient for a covered item if the doctor does not accept assignment of the Medicare claims.

**Living Trust:** A trust established during one's lifetime to hold property.

**Living Will:** Legal document addressed to a health-care provider, which specifies that artificial life-sustaining measures should not be used when in a *terminal condition.*

**Marital Deduction Trust:** A trust that receives property from the first spouse to die, which is eligible for the marital deduction. The second spouse receives income for life and has unlimited power over the property.

**Medallion Guarantee:** A stamp issued by federally insured banks, credit unions, major brokerage firms on a document, which ensures that the signer is the owner or authorized representative.

**Medicaid Trust:** A trust established by a person receiving public assistance to hold property, to enable the recipient to qualify for aid. Recent laws have severely restricted the use of Medicaid trusts.

**Medigap Insurance:** Insurance policies designed to cover health-care expenses not paid for by Medicare.

**Minor:** A person who has not attained the age of majority (generally eighteen). For example, in Illinois a person is a minor under age eighteen except for purposes of the Illinois Transfers to Minors Act, where a person is considered a minor until the age of twenty-one.

**Nuncupative Will:** An oral will, not recognized in most states. This is a declaration by the testator in his last sickness before a number of witnesses, which is later reduced to writing.

**Oath of Office:** A form of attestation by a person who agrees to carry out duties faithfully.

**[Order Admitting Will to Probate and Appointing Representative]**

**Order Declaring Heirship:** A written declaration of the probate court as to the individuals entitled to inherit from the estate.

**Payable-on-Death (POD) Account:** A designation used by banks and other financial institutions on the disposition of accounts when the owner dies. It does not give the designated recipient any rights to the account while the owner is alive, and the account is included in the owner's estate. The funds avoid having to go through probate.

**Payable-on-Death Designation Form:** Form used by banks to designate the person entitled to receive the account during his lifetime and the person entitled to receive the account upon the death of the original recipient.

**Pecuniary Legacy:** A gift of money by a will.

**Per Capita:** A method of distributing property whereby persons are counted individually without regard to lineal descent. (Latin, meaning "by the head.")

**Per Stirpes:** A method of distributing property whereby persons are counted with regard to lineal descent. (Latin, meaning "by the root.") Assume, for example, that I have three children and one child marries and has two children, another has three children, and the third has four children. If I distribute my property to my grandchildren per stirpes, each family unit would receive one third. If I distribute my property per capita, the first family unit would receive ⅖, the second unit would receive ⅗, and the last would receive ⅘.

**Plenary Guardianship:** Full guardianship over a person's financial or personal affairs when limited guardianship would not provide sufficient protection for a disabled person and his estate.

**Pooled-Income Fund:** A trust established and operated by a charity whereby a donor can make a gift of funds to the trust and receive payments based on the earnings in the fund. The donor receives a charitable deduction on his income-tax return.

**Posthumous Child:** A child born after the death of the father.

**Power of Appointment:** A grant of authority in a will or trust over property. It may result in the property being included in that person's estate. If a general power of appointment is in existence and not subject to a contingency at death, that property will be included in the gross estate for federal estate-tax purposes of the holder of the power. The nature of the agent's rights is determined in accordance with state law. See Treasury Regulation 20.2041 and TAM 9722001, 7/12/96.

**Power of Attorney:** Legal document whereby an individual grants another the authority to act on her behalf. A durable power of attorney (must conform to specific language in statutes) remains valid even if the principal becomes incompetent.

**Probate:** Generally, the process of transferring a decedent's property by a court and winding up the affairs of an estate. A probate court has jurisdiction over an incompetent person's welfare during his lifetime.

**Probate Property:** Property interests subject to the court's jurisdiction. Generally excludes insurance policies, individual retirement accounts, deferred compensation plans, property in trusts, annuities, and jointly held property. Include causes of action (such as lawsuits), and all property held in the decedent's name alone.

**Qualified Domestic Trust (QDOT):** A trust allowed by §2056A of the Internal Revenue Code for decedents whose spouses are not U.S. citizens.

**Qualified Family-Owned Business Interest:** The Taxpayer Relief Act of 1997 added new §2033A to allow an exclusion from estate tax of a QFOBI. The maximum exclusion is $675,000 in 1998. This exclusion is for a trade or business with its principal place of business in the United States, with various requirements.

**Qualified Funeral Trust:** A trust allowed to accept property for burial expenses of a decedent. The trust property is not included in the estate.

**Qualified Personal-Residence Trust (QPRT):** A trust for a personal residence (and related structures) for the benefit of family members, which can result in significant estate-tax savings. See Treasury Regulation §25.2702-5.

**Qualified Terminal-Interest Property (QTIP):** (Also known as C Trust.) A trust into which decedent's property that qualifies for the unlimited marital deduction is transferred. The trust pays trust income annually to the surviving spouse for her life, and trust principal to beneficiaries designated by the decedent upon her death. The surviving spouse has only limited access to trust principal and the principal is included in her estate. Generally used with second marriages to protect children from a first marriage.

**Rabbi Trust:** Name for a type of IRS-approved deferred-compensation arrangement. The employer establishes an irrevocable trust for the purpose of holding employee-deferred compensation.

**Remainder Interest:** The right to receive income or property when a life estate in the income or property terminates. A person who owns a fee-simple interest in a piece of property can transfer the remainder interest in his property.

**Residuary Clause:** A provision in a will that directs distribution of decedent's property if all named beneficiaries are deceased or the will fails to distribute all property.

**Reverse Mortgage:** A loan from a bank whereby the bank pays an individual monthly payments while he remains in possession of his house. The loan is due when he dies or moves. Generally not favored, due to high initial loan costs.

**Reverse QTIP:** Name for an election under §2652(a)(3) to treat property held in a QTIP trust as though it were not held in the trust and qualified for the generation skipping transfer tax exemption.

**Reversion:** An interest in real property that returns to the grantor upon the occurrence or nonoccurrence of an event.

**Reversionary Interest:** A right to a future interest in property currently owned by someone else.

**Revival:** Giving new life to a will or trust that had previously been canceled by a subsequent will or trust.

**Revocation:** The act of voiding a will by destroying the document or executing a new will that cancels the old will.

**Roth IRA:** A type of individual retirement account that allows accumulated earnings to grow tax-exempt; contributions are not deductible; there are adjusted-gross-earnings limitations on individuals who qualify for the account; there are possible penalty-free distributions prior to age 59½.

**Rule Against Perpetuities:** A favorite among law students. The law disfavors restrictions on real property (land and things affixed to land) that last indefinitely. A restriction placed on property may not last beyond a period extending the greater of a life or lives in being plus twenty-one years (plus gestation period). This means I cannot draft a trust that will last after my youngest grandchild's life plus twenty-one years. A violation of this rule may void a will, trust, or a part thereof.

**Second-to-Die Life-Insurance Policy:** An insurance policy payable after the second owner dies.

**Section 2503(c) Trust:** A trust for the benefit of minors allowed under this section of the Internal Revenue Code. Sometimes a better gifting technique than the Uniform Gift to Minor's Act, since the trust may continue after the minor reaches age 21.

**Self-Canceling Installment Note:** A written obligation (debt) that is cancelled (forgiven) upon the death of the holder of the note.

**Small Estate Affidavit:** Document that can be used in lieu of probate to transfer title to property (Illinois) when the decedent has less than $50,000 in personal property.

**Special Needs Trust:** A trust established for the benefit of individuals with disabilities for their future health and welfare.

**Spend Down:** Rules established by public assistance to prevent persons from disposing of their assets to enable them to qualify for benefits.

**Spendthrift Trust:** A trust designed to provide a beneficiary a limited amount of money when a person is unable to manage money. The trustee provides funds when the beneficiary needs money in accordance with the terms of the trust agreement. Trust funds are generally not attachable by creditors.

**Split Gift:** A gift made by one spouse to any other person besides his spouse is considered made one-half by each spouse, provided each spouse is a citizen or resident of the United States. The consenting spouse's signature must appear on line 18 of the Form 709, United States Gift (and Generation-Skipping Transfer) Tax Return.

**Sprinkling Trust:** An irrevocable trust where the trustee has the power to designate the amounts that each beneficiary will receive in accordance with the agreement.

**Stepped-Up Basis:** Increase in the tax basis of property inherited due to the death of the owner. Property of a decedent is increased to its fair market value on the date of death or alternate valuation date (if so chosen by the executor). If you inherit stock that cost the decedent $20 per share, and it has a fair market value of $100 on the date of his death, you have a tax basis in the shares of $100, not $20. If you later sell the stock, you pay gain on the difference between $100 and the selling price. There is an exception for property transferred to the decedent and then inherited within one year.

**[Supervised Administration]**

**Supplemental Security Income (SSI) Trust:** A trust established for a disabled person to provide income that will supplement his public assistance.

**Surety Bond:** A bond based on the amount of personal property in an estate that an executor or administrator may be required to post with the probate court to secure creditors and beneficiaries against loss caused by improper administration of the estate.

**Temporary Guardianship:** Responsibility over the personal and financial affairs of a minor or disabled person for a limited time.

**Tenancy in Common:** Form of ownership in real estate, whereby two or more persons hold ownership interests in the same property.

**Tenancy by Entirety:** Form of ownership for married couples whereby each has an undivided interest in the property with rights of survivorship.

**Terminable Interest:** An interest in property that ceases based on the passage of time or occurrence or nonoccurrence of an event. See Treasury Regulation 20.2056(b)-1. No marital deduction is allowed for property with a terminable interest, such as life estates, term for years, annuities, patents, and copyrights.

**Terminal Condition:** An illness or injury for which there is no reasonable prospect of recovery; death is imminent.

**Terminal Interest:** A right in property that ends at a certain time or when a contingency occurs or fails to occur.

**Testate:** A person who dies leaving a valid will.

**Testator:** Maker of a will; if female, called Testatrix.

**Testamentary Trust:** A trust funded by a will; comes into existence at death. Trust often can be found in the same document as the will.

**Totten Trust:** Method that avoids probate; used at financial institutions where an account holder designates an individual who is to receive the account upon the depositor's death; not really a trust. The balance in the account is included in the decedent's estate.

**Transfer-on-Death Designations:** Forms completed by owners of accounts designating who will receive the account upon the death of the owner.

**Trustee:** Person or corporation holding title to property for the benefit of another.

**Trustor:** Person who established a trust.

**Unified Credit:** A nonrefundable credit against federal estate taxes, which allows each person to transfer a certain amount either by gift during their lifetime or at death. The exclusion amount times the tax rate equals the amount of tax credit allowed.

| Date of Death | Tax Credit | Property Exclusion Amount |
| --- | --- | --- |
| 1998 | 202,050 | 625,000 |
| 1999 | 211,300 | 650,000 |
| 2000–2001 | 220,550 | 675,000 |
| 2002–2003 | 229,800 | 700,000 |
| 2004 | 287,300 | 850,000 |
| 2005 | 326,300 | 950,000 |
| after 2005 | 345,800 | 1,000,000 |

**Uniform Gifts or Transfers to Minor's Acts:** Laws established by the states to allow persons to transfer property to a trustee to be held until the minor reaches the age of majority.

**Uniform Probate Code:** A set of rules and laws adopted by the states regarding decedent's estates.

**Unlimited Marital Deduction:** Property transferred to a spouse at death and deducted from the gross estate in determining estate tax-liability. The marital deduction is unlimited, so generally there will be no federal estate tax due when the first spouse dies if all property is transferred to the surviving spouse. Not a good planning technique when used alone for larger estates, since both spouses will not utilize their unified credit.

**Ward:** A minor or disabled person whose welfare is under the jurisdiction of the court.

**Will:** Legal document that takes effect upon the death of the testator, which expresses his intentions regarding his property and children.

# Common Estate Acronyms

| | |
|---|---|
| AGI | Adjusted Gross Income |
| CRT | Charitable Remainder Trust |
| DNI | Distributable Net Income |
| DNR | Do Not Resuscitate order |
| DRD | Deductions in Respect of a Decedent |
| EIN | Employer Identification Number |
| ESBT | Electing Small Business Trust |
| ESOP | Employee Stock Ownership Plan |
| GRAT | Grantor Retained Annuity Trust |
| GRIT | Grantor Retained Income Trust |
| GRUT | Grantor Retained Unitrust |
| GSTT | Generation-Skipping-Transfer Tax |
| HCFA | Health-Care Financing Administration |
| IRA | Individual Retirement Account |
| IRC | Internal Revenue Code |
| IRD | Income in Respect of a Decedent |
| IRS | Internal Revenue Service |
| LLC | Limited Liability Company |
| LOA | Letter of Authorization |
| LTC | Long-Term Care insurance |
| MSA | Medical Savings Account |
| NOL | Net Operating Loss |
| PLR | Private Letter Ruling |

| | |
|---|---|
| POA | Power of Attorney |
| POD | Payable-on-Death account |
| QFT | Qualified Funeral Trust |
| QDOT | Qualified Domestic Trust |
| QDRO | Qualified Domestic Relations Order |
| QFOBI | Qualified Family-Owned Business Interest |
| QPRT | Qualified Personal Residence Trust |
| QSST | Qualified Subchapter S Trust |
| QSTP | Qualified State Tuition Program |
| QTIP | Qualified Terminal-Interest Property |
| RRA | Railroad Retirement Act |
| RRB | Railroad Retirement Board |
| SSA | Social Security Administration |
| UGMA | Uniform Gift to Minor's Act |

C

# Federal Estate- and Gift-Tax Rates

## I.R.C. §2001(C)(1)

The federal estate- and gift-tax rate is a unified rate on the transfer of property from one person to another either during the person's lifetime or at death. The unified credit amount to which each person is entitled can be used up during his lifetime, when he makes taxable gifts. The unified concept is necessary to prevent a person from gifting away all of her wealth prior to her death.

| | |
|---|---|
| Not over $10,000 | 18% |
| Over $10,000 but not over $20,000 | $1,800 + 20% of amount over $10,000 |
| Over $20,000 but not over $40,000 | $3,800 + 22% of amount over $20,000 |
| Over $40,000 but not over $60,000 | $8,200 + 24% of amount over $40,000 |
| Over $60,000 but not over $80,000 | $13,000 + 26% of amount over $60,000 |
| Over $80,000 but not over $100,000 | $18,200 + 28% of amount over $80,000 |
| Over $100,000 but not over $150,000 | $23,800 + 30% of amount over $100,000 |

| | |
|---|---|
| Over $150,000 but not over $250,000 | $38,800 + 32% of amount over $150,000 |
| Over $250,000 but not over $500,000 | $70,800 + 34% of amount over $250,000 |
| Over $500,000 but not over $750,000 | $155,800 + 37% of amount over $500,000 |
| Over $750,000 but not over $1,000,000 | $248,300 + 39% of amount over $750,000 |
| Over $1,000,000 but not over $1,250,000 | $345,800 + 41% of amount over $1,000,000 |
| Over $1,250,000 but not over $1,500,000 | $448,300 + 43% of amount over $1,250,000 |
| Over $1,500,000 but not over $2,000,000 | $555,800 + 45% of amount over $1,500,000 |
| Over $2,000,000 but not over $2,500,000 | $780,800 + 49% of amount over $2,000,000 |
| Over $2,500,000 but not over $3,000,000 | $1,025,800 + 53% of amount over $2,500,000 |
| Over $3,000,000 | $1,290,800 + 55% of amount over $3,000,000 |

The unified-credit amount and the above graduated rates are reduced by 5 percent of the taxable estate over $10,000,000 but not over $21,040,000. Internal Revenue Code §2001(c)(2).

## GENERATION-SKIPPING-TRANSFER TAX RATES
## I.R.C. §2641

The applicable rate is the product of the maximum federal estate- and gift-tax rate for decedent's dying on the date of the taxable distribution, termination, or direct skip, and the inclusion ratio. The inclusion ratio, defined in §2642, is a calculated percentage based on the amount of property transferred in a generation-skipping transfer and the amount of the exemption allocated to the transfer.

## FEDERAL INCOME TAX RATES FOR ESTATES AND TRUSTS
## I.R.C. §1(E)

| If taxable income is over: | The tax is: |
| --- | --- |
| Not over $1,500 | 15% of taxable income |
| Over $1,500 but not over $3,500 | $225, plus 28% of the excess over $1,500 |
| Over $3,500 but not over $5,500 | $785, plus 31% of the excess over $3,500 |
| Over $5,500 but not over $7,500 | $1,405, plus 36% of the excess over $5,500 |
| Over $7,500 | $2,125, plus 39.6% of the excess over $1,500 |

# D

# Information Sources

There are many local, county, city, state, and national organizations, which provide assistance free of charge. Most have free brochures to explain their services. Check with your local probate court clerk to find out if they have handouts or where you can purchase copies of the local rules. Contact your secretary of state's office for brochures on transferring titles to cars, boats, etc. If you suspect an elderly person is in need of assistance, contact the local county health departments; they will know which agency has jurisdiction.

## ALZHEIMER ASSOCIATION

Information on Alzheimer disease and related disorders.

1-800-272-3900
919 N. Michigan Avenue
Suite 1000
Chicago, Illinois 60611

## DEPARTMENT OF EDUCATION

Information on affording college, obtaining student aid, such as Pell grants and student loans.

1-800-USA-LEARN
*http://www.ed.gov/prog_info/SFA/StudentGuide*

## FEDERAL DEPOSIT INSURANCE CORPORATION

Verify that your bank, financial institution, money-market accounts are federally insured against loss.

1-800-934-3342

*www.fdic.gov*

## HEALTH-CARE FINANCING ADMINISTRATION

Agency responsible for oversight of Medicare, the federal portion of Medicaid, and related activities.

Administrator
Health-Care Financing Administration
Department of Health and Human Services
200 Independence Avenue SW
Washington, DC 20201

## ILLINOIS INSURANCE DEPARTMENT

Illinois agency with responsibility to enforce state laws; provides information on insurance.

Insurance Department
320 West Washington Street
4th Floor
Springfield, IL 62767

## INTERNAL REVENUE SERVICE

Free tax preparation assistance through their excellent VITA (Volunteer Income Tax Assistance) program. There are numerous free publications on every aspect of taxes. To order forms, call 1-800-829-3676.

## NATIONAL ASSOCIATION OF INSURANCE COMMISSIONERS

Organization that will provide an informative brochure on Long-Term-Care insurance.

NAIC
120 West 12th Street
Suite 1100
Kansas City, MO 64105-1925

## NATIONAL ELDERCARE LOCATOR SERVICE
Service run by the National Association of Area Agencies on Aging. A hotline number provides the names of local agencies that help seniors find housing.
1-800-677-1116
NELC
1112 16th Street NW
Suite 100
Washington, DC 20036

## PENSION BENEFIT GUARANTY CORPORATION
Government-owned corporation that insures most private sector defined-benefit pension plans.
PBGC
1200 K Street NW
Washington, DC 20005-4026

## RAILROAD RETIREMENT BOARD
Provides sickness, unemployment, and pension benefits to the nation's railroad workers covered under the Railroad Retirement Act.
RRB
844 North Rush Street
Chicago, IL 60611

## SOCIAL SECURITY ADMINISTRATION
Agency that pays social security and other benefits. They will provide individual benefit and account information.
1-800-772-1213
*http://www.ssa.gov*

## U.S. BUSINESS ADVISOR
Excellent Web site for frequently asked questions about government services.
*http://www.business.gov*

## U.S. SAVINGS BOND INFORMATION

Information and brochures on various issues to include the Education
Bond Program.

*http://www.publicdebt.treas.gov*
Bureau of the Public Debt
Savings Bonds Marketing Office
Washington, DC 20226

# Sample Durable Power of Attorney for Property

[NOTICE: THE PURPOSE OF THIS
POWER OF ATTORNEY IS TO GIVE
THE PERSON YOU DESIGNATE
(YOUR AGENT) BROAD POWERS
TO HANDLE YOUR PROPERTY,
WHICH MAY INCLUDE POWERS
TO PLEDGE, SELL, OR OTHERWISE
DISPOSE OF ANY REAL OR
PERSONAL PROPERTY WITHOUT
ADVANCE NOTICE TO YOU OR
APPROVAL BY YOU. THIS FORM

DOES NOT IMPOSE A DUTY ON YOUR
AGENT TO EXERCISE GRANTED POWERS;

(Above space for Recorder's use only)

BUT WHEN POWERS ARE EXERCISED, YOUR AGENT WILL HAVE
TO USE DUE CARE TO ACT FOR YOUR BENEFIT AND IN ACCOR-
DANCE WITH THIS FORM AND KEEP A RECORD OF RECEIPTS,
DISBURSEMENTS, AND SIGNIFICANT ACTIONS TAKEN AS AGENT.
A COURT CAN TAKE AWAY THE POWERS OF YOUR AGENT IF IT
FINDS THE AGENT IS NOT ACTING PROPERLY. YOU MAY NAME
SUCCESSOR AGENTS UNDER THIS FORM BUT NO COAGENTS,
UNLESS YOU EXPRESSLY LIMIT THE DURATION OF THIS POWER
IN THE MANNER PROVIDED BELOW. UNTIL YOU REVOKE THIS

POWER OR A COURT ACTING ON YOUR BEHALF TERMINATES IT, YOUR AGENT MAY EXERCISE THE POWERS GIVEN HERE THROUGHOUT YOUR LIFETIME, EVEN AFTER YOU BECOME DISABLED. THE POWERS YOU GIVE YOUR AGENT ARE EXPLAINED MORE FULLY IN §3-4 OF THE ILLINOIS "STATUTORY SHORT-FORM POWER OF ATTORNEY FOR PROPERTY LAW" OF WHICH THIS FORM IS A PART (SEE THE BACK OF THIS FORM). THAT LAW EXPRESSLY PERMITS THE USE OF ANY DIFFERENT FORM OF POWER OF ATTORNEY YOU MAY DESIRE. IF THERE IS ANYTHING ABOUT THIS FORM THAT YOU DO NOT UNDERSTAND, YOU SHOULD ASK A LAWYER TO EXPLAIN IT TO YOU.]

POWER OF ATTORNEY made this _____ day of _____, _____.

1.  I, _____

(name and address of principal)

hereby appoint:

_____

(name and address of agent)

as my attorney-in-fact (my "agent") to act for me and in my name (in any way I could act in person) with respect to the following powers, as defined in §3-4 of the "Statutory Short-Form Power of Attorney Law" (including amendments), but subject to any limitations on or additions to the specified powers inserted in paragraph 2 or 3 below:

(YOU MUST STRIKE OUT ANY ONE OR MORE OF THE FOLLOWING CATEGORIES OF POWERS YOU DO NOT WANT YOUR AGENT TO HAVE, FAILURE TO STRIKE THE TITLE OF ANY CATEGORY WILL CAUSE THE POWERS DESCRIBED IN THAT CATEGORY TO BE GRANTED TO THE AGENT. TO STRIKE OUT A CATEGORY YOU MUST DRAW A LINE THROUGH THE TITLE OF THAT CATEGORY.)

(a)     Real estate transactions
(b)     Financial institution transactions
(c)     Stock and bond transactions
(d)     Tangible personal property transactions
(e)     Safe-deposit-box transactions
(f)     Insurance and annuity transactions
(g)     Retirement plan transactions

(h)    Social Security, employment, and military-service benefits
(i)    Tax matters
(j)    Claims and litigation
(k)    Commodity and option transactions
(l)    Business operations
(m)    Borrowing transactions
(n)    Estate transactions
(o)    All other property powers and transactions

(LIMITATIONS ON AND ADDITIONS TO THE AGENT'S POWERS MAY BE INCLUDED IN THIS POWER OF ATTORNEY IF THEY ARE SPECIFICALLY DESCRIBED BELOW.)

2. The powers granted above shall not include the following powers or shall be modified or limited in the following particulars (HERE YOU MAY INCLUDE ANY SPECIFIC LIMITATIONS YOU DEEM APPROPRIATE, SUCH AS PROHIBITION OR CONDITIONS ON THE SALE OF PARTICULAR STOCK OR REAL ESTATE OR SPECIAL RULES ON BORROWING BY THE AGENT):

_____

_____

_____

3. In addition to the powers granted above, I grant my agent the following powers (HERE YOU MAY ADD ANY OTHER DELEGATABLE POWERS INCLUDING, WITHOUT LIMITATION, POWER TO MAKE GIFTS, EXERCISE POWERS OF APPOINTMENT, NAME OR CHANGE BENEFICIARIES OR JOINT TENANTS OR REVOKE OR AMEND ANY TRUST SPECIFICALLY REFERRED TO BELOW):

_____

_____

_____

(YOUR AGENT WILL HAVE AUTHORITY TO EMPLOY OTHER PERSONS AS NECESSARY TO ENABLE THE AGENT TO PROPERLY EXERCISE THE POWERS GRANTED IN THIS FORM, BUT YOUR AGENT WILL HAVE TO MAKE ALL DISCRETIONARY DECISIONS. IF YOU WANT TO GIVE YOUR AGENT THE RIGHT TO DELEGATE DIS-

CRETIONARY DECISION-MAKING POWERS TO OTHERS, YOU SHOULD KEEP THE NEXT SENTENCE, OTHERWISE IT SHOULD BE STRUCK OUT.)

4. My agent shall have the right by written instrument to delegate any or all of the foregoing powers involving discretionary decision-making to any person or persons whom my agent may select, but such delegation may be amended or revoked by any agent (including any successor) named by me who is acting under this power of attorney at the time of reference.

(YOUR AGENT WILL BE ENTITLED TO REIMBURSEMENT FOR ALL REASONABLE EXPENSES INCURRED IN ACTING UNDER THIS POWER OF ATTORNEY. STRIKE OUT THE NEXT SENTENCE IF YOU DO NOT WANT YOUR AGENT TO ALSO BE ENTITLED TO REA- SONABLE COMPENSATION FOR SERVICES AS AGENT.)

5. My agent shall be entitled to reasonable compensation for services rendered as agent under this power of attorney.

(THIS POWER OF ATTORNEY MAY BE AMENDED OR REVOKED BY YOU AT ANY TIME AND IN ANY MANNER. ABSENT AMENDMENT OR REVOCATION, THE AUTHORITY GRANTED IN THIS POWER OF ATTORNEY WILL BECOME EFFECTIVE AT THE TIME THIS POWER IS SIGNED AND WILL CONTINUE UNTIL YOUR DEATH UNLESS A LIMITATION ON THE BEGINNING DATE OR DURATION IS MADE BY INITIALING AND COMPLETING EITHER [OR BOTH] OF THE FOLLOWING:)

6. ( ) This power of attorney shall become effective on

_____.

(INSERT A FUTURE DATE OR EVENT DURING YOUR LIFETIME, SUCH AS COURT DETERMINATION OF YOUR DISABILITY, WHEN YOU WANT THIS POWER TO FIRST TAKE EFFECT.)

7. ( ) This power of attorney shall terminate on

_____.

(INSERT A FUTURE DATE OR EVENT DURING YOUR LIFETIME, SUCH AS COURT DETERMINATION OF YOUR DISABILITY, WHEN YOU WANT THIS POWER TO TERMINATE PRIOR TO YOUR DEATH.)

8. If any agent named by me shall die, become incompetent, resign, or refuse to accept the office of agent, I name the following (each to act alone and successively, in the order named) as successor(s) to such agent:

_____

_____

_____

For purposes of this paragraph 8, a person shall be considered to be incompetent, if and while the person is a minor, or an adjudicated incompetent, or disabled person, or the person is unable to give prompt and intelligent consideration to business matters, as certified by a licensed physician.

(IF YOU WISH TO NAME YOUR AGENT AS GUARDIAN OF YOUR ESTATE, IN THE EVENT A COURT DECIDES THAT ONE SHOULD BE APPOINTED, YOU MAY, BUT ARE NOT REQUIRED TO DO SO BY RETAINING THE FOLLOWING PARAGRAPH. THE COURT WILL APPOINT YOUR AGENT IF THE COURT FINDS THAT SUCH APPOINTMENT WILL SERVE YOUR BEST INTERESTS AND WELFARE, STRIKE OUT PARAGRAPH 9 IF YOU DO NOT WANT YOUR AGENT TO ACT AS GUARDIAN.)

9. If a guardian of my estate (my property) is to be appointed, I nominate the agent acting under this power of attorney as such guardian, to serve without bond or security.

10. I am fully informed as to all the contents of this form and understand the full import of this grant of powers to my agent.

Signed _____

(Principal)

(YOU MAY, BUT ARE NOT REQUIRED TO, REQUEST YOUR AGENT AND SUCCESSOR AGENTS TO PROVIDE SPECIMEN SIGNATURES BELOW. IF YOU INCLUDE SPECIMEN SIGNATURES IN THIS POWER

OF ATTORNEY, YOU MUST COMPLETE THE CERTIFICATION
OPPOSITE THE SIGNATURES OF THE AGENTS.)

Specimen signatures of agent     I certify that the signatures of my
(and successors)     agent (and successors) are correct.

_____     _____
(agent)     (principal)

_____     _____
(successor agent)     (principal)

_____     _____
(successor agent)     (principal)

THIS POWER OF ATTORNEY WILL NOT BE EFFECTIVE UNLESS IT
IS NOTARIZED, USING THE FORM BELOW.

State of _____) ss.
County of _____)

The undersigned, a notary public in and for the above county and state,
certifies that _____ known to me to be
the same person whose name is subscribed as principal to the foregoing
power of attorney, appeared before me in person and acknowledged signing and delivering the instrument as the free and voluntary act of the
principal, for the uses and purposes therein set forth (and certified to the
correctness of the signature(s) of the agent(s)).

Dated: _____

(Seal) _____
Notary Public

My commission expires _____

(THE NAME AND ADDRESS OF THE PERSON PREPARING THIS
FORM SHOULD BE INSERTED IF THE AGENT WILL HAVE POWER
TO CONVEY ANY INTEREST IN REAL ESTATE.)

This document was prepared by:

## EXPLANATION OF POWERS GRANTED IN THIS
## POWER OF ATTORNEY FOR PROPERTY

**Section 3-4. Explanation of powers granted in the statutory short form of power of attorney for property.** This section defines each category of powers listed in the statutory short-form power of attorney for property and the effect of granting powers to an agent. When the title of any of the following categories is retained (not struck out) in a statutory property power form, the effect will be to grant the agent all of the principal's rights, powers, and discretions with respect to the types of property and transactions covered by the retained category, subject to any limitations on the granted powers that appear on the face of the form. The agent will have authority to exercise each granted power for and in the name of the principal with respect to all of the principal's interests in every type of property or transaction covered by the granted power at the time of exercise, whether the principal's interests are direct or indirect, in whole or fractional, legal, equitable, or contractual, as a joint tenant or tenant in common or held in any other form; but the agent will not have power under any of the statutory categories (a) through (o) to make gifts of the principal's property, to exercise powers to appoint to others, or to change any beneficiary whom the principal has designated to take the principal's interests at death under any will, trust, joint tenancy, beneficiary form, or contractual arrangement. The agent will be under no duty to exercise granted powers or to assume control of or responsibility for the principal's property or affairs; but when granted powers are exercised, the agent will be required to use due care to act for the benefit of the principal in accordance with the terms of the statutory property power and will be liable for negligent exercise. The agent may act in person or through others reasonably employed by the agent for that purpose and will have authority to sign and deliver all instruments, negotiate and enter into all agreements and do all other acts reasonably necessary to implement the exercise of the powers granted to the agent.

(a) REAL ESTATE TRANSACTIONS. The agent is authorized to: buy, sell, exchange, rent, and lease real estate (which term includes, without limitation, real estate subject to a land trust and all beneficial interest in and powers of direction under any land trust); collect all rent, sale proceeds, and earnings from real estate; convey, assign, and accept title to real estate; grant easements, create conditions, and release rights of homestead with respect to real estate; create land trusts and exercise all powers under land trusts; hold, possess, maintain, repair, improve, subdivide, manage, operate, and insure real estate; pay, contest, protest, and compromise real estate taxes and assessments; and, in general, exercise all powers with respect to real estate which the principal could if present and under no disability.

(b) FINANCIAL INSTITUTION TRANSACTIONS. The agent is authorized to: open, close, continue, and control all accounts and deposits in any type of financial institution (which term includes, without limitation, banks, trust companies, savings and building and loan associations, credit unions, and brokerage firms); deposit in and withdraw from and write checks on any financial institution account or deposit; and, in general, exercise all powers with respect to financial institution transactions which the principal could if present and under no disability.

(c) STOCK AND BOND TRANSACTIONS. The agent is authorized to: buy and sell all types of securities (which term includes, without limitation, stocks, bonds, mutual funds, and all other types of investment securities and financial instruments); collect, hold, and safekeep all dividends, interest, earnings, proceeds of sale, distributions, shares, certificates, and other evidences of ownership paid or distributed with respect to securities, exercise all voting rights with respect to securities in person or by proxy, enter into voting trusts and consent to limitations on the right to vote; and, in general, exercise all powers with respect to securities which the principal could if present and under no disability.

(d) TANGIBLE PERSONAL PROPERTY TRANSACTIONS. The agent is authorized to: buy and sell, lease, exchange, collect, possess, and take title to all tangible personal property; move, store, ship, restore, maintain, repair, improve, manage, preserve, insure, and safekeep tangible personal property; and, in general, exercise all powers with respect to tangible personal property which the principal could if present and under no disability.

(e) SAFE DEPOSIT TRANSACTIONS. The agent is authorized to: continue and have access to all safe-deposit boxes; sign, renew, release, or terminate any safe-deposit contract; drill or surrender any safe-deposit box; and, in general, exercise all powers with respect to safe-deposit box matters which the principal could if present and under no disability.

(f) INSURANCE AND ANNUITY TRANSACTIONS. The agent is authorized to: procure, acquire, continue, renew, terminate, or otherwise deal with any type of insurance or annuity contract (which terms include, without limitation, life, accident, health, disability, automobile casualty, property, or liability insurance); pay premiums or assessments on or surrender and collect all distributions, proceeds or benefits payable under any insurance or annuity contract; and, in general, exercise all powers with respect to insurance and annuity contracts which the principal could if present and under no disability.

(g) RETIREMENT PLAN TRANSACTIONS. The agent is authorized to: contribute to, withdraw from, and deposit funds in any type of retirement plan (which term includes, without limitation, any tax-qualified or non-qualified pension, profit sharing, stock bonus, employee savings, and other retirement plans, individual retirement account, deferred-compensation plan, and any other type of employee-benefit plan); select and change payment options for the principal under any retirement plan; make rollover contributions from any retirement plan to other retirement plans or individual retirement accounts; exercise all investment powers available under any type of self-directed retirement plan; and, in general, exercise all powers with respect to retirement plans and retirement plan account balances which the principal could if present and under no disability.

(h) SOCIAL SECURITY, UNEMPLOYMENT, AND MILITARY-SERVICE BENEFITS. The agent is authorized to: prepare, sign, and file any claim or application for Social Security, unemployment, or military-service benefits; sue for, settle, or abandon any claims to any benefit or assistance under any federal, state, local, or foreign statute or regulation; control, deposit to any account, collect, receipt for, and take title to and hold all benefits under any Social Security, unemployment, military service, or other state, federal, local, or foreign statute or regulation; and, in general, exercise all powers with respect to Social Security, unemployment, military service, and governmental benefits which the principal could if present and under no disability.

(i) TAX MATTERS. The agent is authorized to: sign, verify, and file all the principal's federal, state, and local income, gift, estate, property, and other tax returns, including joint returns and declarations of estimated tax; pay all taxes; claim, sue for, and receive all tax refunds; examine and copy all the principal's tax returns and records; represent the principal before any federal, state, or local revenue agency or taxing body and sign and deliver all tax powers of attorney on behalf of the principal that may be necessary for such purposes; waive rights and sign all documents on behalf of the principal as required to settle, pay, and determine all tax liabilities; and, in general, exercise all powers with respect to tax matters which the principal could if present and under no disability.

(j)  CLAIMS AND LITIGATION. The agent is authorized to: institute, prosecute, defend, abandon, compromise, arbitrate, settle, and dispose of any claim in favor of or against the principal or any property interests of the principal; collect and receipt for any claim or settlement proceeds and waive or release all rights of the principal; employ attorneys and others and enter into contingency agreements and other contracts necessary in connection with litigation; and, in general, exercise all powers with respect to claims and litigation which the principal could if present and under no disability.

(k) COMMODITY AND OPTION TRANSACTIONS. The agent is authorized to: buy, sell, exchange, assign, convey, settle, and exercise commodities futures contracts and call and put options on stocks and stock indices traded on a regulated options exchange, and collect and receipt for all proceeds of any such transactions; establish or continue option accounts for the principal with any securities or futures broker; and, in general, exercise all powers with respect to commodities and options which the principal could if present and under no disability.

(l)  BUSINESS OPERATIONS. The agent is authorized to: organize or continue and conduct any business (which term includes, without limitation, any farming, manufacturing, service, mining, retailing, or other type of business operation) in any form, whether as a proprietorship, joint venture, partnership, corporation, trust or other legal entity; operate, buy, sell, expand, contract, terminate, or liquidate any business; direct, control, supervise, manage, or participate in the operation of any business; and engage, compensate, and discharge business managers, employees, agents, attorneys, accountants, and consultants; and, in general, exercise all powers with respect to business interests and operations which the principal could if present and under no disability.

(m)      BORROWING TRANSACTIONS. The agent is authorized to: borrow money; mortgage or pledge any real estate or tangible or intangible personal property as security for such purposes; sign, renew, extend, pay, and satisfy any notes or other forms of obligation; and, in general, exercise all powers with respect to secured and unsecured borrowing which the principal could if present and under no disability.

(n) ESTATE TRANSACTIONS. The agent is authorized to: accept, receipt for, exercise, release, reject, renounce, assign, disclaim, demand, sue for, claim, and recover any legacy, bequest, devise, gift, or other property interest or payment due or payable to or for the principal; assert any interest in and exercise any power over any trust, estate or property subject to fiduciary control; establish a revocable trust solely for the benefit of the principal that terminates at the death of the principal and is then distributable to the legal representatives of the estate of the principal; and, in general, exercise all powers with respect to estate and trusts which the principal could if present and under no disability; provided, however, that the agent may not make or change a will and may not revoke or amend a trust revocable or amendable by the principal or require the trustee of any trust for the benefit of the principal to pay income or principal to the agent unless specific authority to the end is given, and specific reference to the trust is made, in the statutory property power form.

(o) ALL OTHER PROPERTY POWERS AND TRANSACTIONS. The agent is authorized to: exercise all possible powers of the principal with respect to all possible types of property and interests in property, except to the extent the principal limits the generality of this category (o) by striking out one or more categories (a) through (n) or by specifying other limitations in the statutory property power form.

# Sample Statutory Short-Form Power of Attorney for Health Care

755 ILCS 45/4-10(a) effective January 1993

[NOTICE: THE PURPOSE OF THIS POWER OF ATTORNEY IS TO GIVE THE PERSON YOU DESIGNATE (YOUR AGENT) BROAD POWERS TO MAKE HEALTH-CARE DECISIONS FOR YOU, INCLUDING POWER TO REQUIRE, CONSENT TO, OR WITHDRAW ANY TYPE OF PERSONAL CARE OR MEDICAL TREATMENT FOR ANY PHYSICAL OR MENTAL CONDITION AND TO ADMIT YOU TO OR DISCHARGE YOU FROM ANY HOSPITAL, HOME, OR OTHER INSTITUTION. THIS FORM DOES NOT IMPOSE A DUTY ON YOUR AGENT TO EXERCISE GRANTED POWERS; BUT WHEN POWERS ARE EXERCISED, YOUR AGENT WILL HAVE TO USE DUE CARE TO ACT FOR YOUR BENEFIT AND IN ACCORDANCE WITH THIS FORM AND KEEP A RECORD OF RECEIPTS, DISBURSEMENTS, AND SIGNIFICANT ACTIONS TAKEN UNDER THIS FORM BUT NOT COAGENTS, AND NO HEALTH CARE PROVIDER MAY BE NAMED UNLESS YOU EXPRESSLY LIMIT THE DURATION OF THIS POWER IN THE MANNER PROVIDED BELOW. UNTIL YOU REVOKE THIS POWER OR A COURT ACTING ON YOUR BEHALF TERMINATES IT, YOUR AGENT MAY EXERCISE THE POWERS GIVEN HERE THROUGHOUT YOUR LIFETIME, EVEN AFTER YOU BECOME DISABLED. THE POWERS YOU GIVE YOUR AGENT, YOUR RIGHT TO REVOKE THOSE POWERS AND THE PENALTIES FOR VIOLATING THE LAW ARE

EXPLAINED MORE FULLY IN §§4-5, 4-6, 4-9, AND 4-10(B) OF THE ILLINOIS "POWERS OF ATTORNEY FOR HEALTH-CARE LAW" OF WHICH THIS FORM IS A PART. THAT LAW EXPRESSLY PERMITS THE USE OF ANY DIFFERENT FORM OF POWER OF ATTORNEY YOU MAY DESIRE. IF THERE IS ANYTHING IN THIS DOCUMENT THAT YOU DO NOT UNDERSTAND, YOU SHOULD CONSULT A LAWYER.]

POWER OF ATTORNEY made this _____ day of _____, _____.

1.  I, _____

(Name of Principal)

hereby appoint:

_____

(Name of Agent)

as my attorney-in-fact (my "agent") to act for me and in my name (in any way I could act in person) to make any and all decisions for me concerning my personal care, medical treatment, hospitalization, and health care and to require, withhold, or withdraw any type of medical treatment or procedure even though my death may ensue. My agent shall have the same access to my medical records that I have, including the right to disclose the contents to others. My agent shall also have full power to make a disposition of any part or all of my body for medical purposes, authorize and direct the disposition of my remains.

(THE ABOVE POWER IS INTENDED TO BE AS BROAD AS POSSIBLE SO THAT YOUR AGENT WILL HAVE AUTHORITY TO MAKE ANY DECISION YOU COULD MAKE TO OBTAIN OR TERMINATE ANY TYPE OF HEALTH CARE, INCLUDING WITHDRAWAL OF FOOD AND WATER AND OTHER LIFE-SUSTAINING MEASURES, IF YOUR AGENT BELIEVES SUCH ACTION WOULD BE CONSISTENT WITH YOUR INTENT AND DESIRES. IF YOU WISH TO LIMIT THE SCOPE OF YOUR AGENT'S POWERS OR PRESCRIBE SPECIAL RULES OR LIMIT THE POWER TO MAKE AN ANATOMICAL GIFT, AUTHORIZE AUTOPSY, OR DISPOSE OF REMAINS, YOU MAY DO SO IN THE FOLLOWING PARAGRAPHS.)

2.   The powers granted above shall not include the following powers or shall be subject to the following rules limitations (HERE YOU MAY INCLUDE ANY SPECIFIC LIMITATIONS YOU DEEM APPROPRIATE, SUCH AS YOUR OWN DEFINITION OF WHEN LIFE-SUSTAINING MEASURES SHOULD BE WITHHELD; A DIRECTION TO CONTINUE FOOD AND FLUIDS OR LIFE-SUSTAINING TREATMENT IN ALL EVENTS; OR INSTRUCTIONS TO REFUSE ANY SPECIFIC TYPES OF TREATMENT THAT ARE INCONSISTENT WITH YOUR RELIGIOUS BELIEFS OR UNACCEPTABLE TO YOU FOR ANY OTHER REASON, SUCH AS BLOOD TRANSFUSIONS, ELECTRO-CONVULSIVE THERAPY, AMPUTATION, PSYCHOSURGERY, VOLUNTARY ADMISSION TO A MENTAL INSTITUTION, ETC.)

(THE SUBJECT OF LIFE-SUSTAINING TREATMENT IS OF PARTICULAR IMPORTANCE. IN DEALING WITH THAT SUBJECT, SOME GENERAL STATEMENTS CONCERNING THE WITHHOLDING OR REMOVAL OF LIFE-SUSTAINING TREATMENT ARE SET FORTH BELOW. IF YOU AGREE WITH ONE OF THESE STATEMENTS, YOU MAY INITIAL THAT STATEMENT; BUT DO NOT INITIAL MORE THAN ONE.)

_____ I do not want my life to be prolonged nor do I want life-sustaining treatment to be provided or continued if my agent believes the burdens of the treatment outweigh the expected benefits. I want my agent to consider the relief of suffering, the expense involved, and the quality as well as the possible extension of my life in making decisions concerning life-sustaining treatment.

_____ I want my life to be prolonged and I want life-sustaining treatment to be provided or continued unless I am in a coma, which my attending physician believes to be irreversible, in accordance with reasonable medical standards at the time of reference. If and when I have suffered irreversible coma, I want life-sustaining treatment to be withheld or discontinued.

_____ I want my life to be prolonged to the greatest extent possible without regard to my condition, the chances I have for recovery, or the cost of the procedures.

(THIS POWER OF ATTORNEY MAY BE AMENDED OR REVOKED BY YOU IN THE MANNER PROVIDED IN §4-6 OF THE ILLINOIS POWERS OF ATTORNEY FOR HEALTH-CARE LAW. ABSENT AMENDMENT OR REVOCATION, THE AUTHORITY GRANTED IN THIS POWER OF ATTORNEY WILL BECOME EFFECTIVE AT THE TIME THIS POWER IS SIGNED AND WILL CONTINUE UNTIL YOUR DEATH AND BEYOND, IF ANATOMICAL GIFT, AUTOPSY, OR DISPOSITION OF REMAINS IS AUTHORIZED, UNLESS A LIMITATION ON THE BEGINNING DATE OR DURATION IS MADE BY INITIALING AND COMPLETING EITHER OR BOTH OF THE FOLLOWING:)

3.   ( ) This Power of Attorney shall become effective on _____.

4.   ( ) This Power of Attorney shall terminate on _____.

(IF YOU WISH TO NAME SUCCESSOR AGENTS, INSERT THE NAMES AND ADDRESSES OF SUCH SUCCESSORS IN THE FOLLOWING PARAGRAPH.)

5.   If any agent named by me shall die, become incompetent, resign, refuse to accept the office of agent, or be unavailable, I name the following (each to act alone and successively, in the order named) as successors to such agent:

_____

_____

For purposes of this paragraph 5, a person shall be considered to be incompetent if and while the person is a minor, or an adjudicated incompetent, or disabled person, or the person is unable to give prompt and intelligent consideration to health-care matters, as certified by a licensed physician.

(IF YOU WISH TO NAME YOUR AGENT AS GUARDIAN OF YOUR PERSON, IN THE EVENT A COURT DECIDES THAT ONE SHOULD BE APPOINTED, YOU MAY BUT ARE NOT REQUIRED TO DO SO BY RETAINING THE FOLLOWING PARAGRAPH. THE COURT WILL APPOINT YOUR AGENT IF THE COURT FINDS THAT SUCH APPOINTMENT WILL SERVE YOUR BEST INTERESTS AND WELFARE. STRIKE OUT PARAGRAPH 6 IF YOU DO NOT WANT YOUR AGENT TO ACT AS GUARDIAN.)

6.  If a guardian of my person is to be appointed, I nominate the agent acting under this Power of Attorney as such guardian, to serve without bond or security.

7.  I am fully informed as to all the contents of this form and understand the full import of this grant of powers to my agent.

_____
(Principal)

_____
(Date)

The principal has had an opportunity to read the above form and has signed the form or acknowledged h_____ signature of mark on the form in my presence.

_____        _____
Witness                               Address

(YOU MAY BUT ARE NOT REQUIRED TO REQUEST YOUR AGENT AND SUCCESSOR AGENTS TO PROVIDE SPECIMEN SIGNATURES BELOW. IF YOU INCLUDE SPECIMEN SIGNATURES IN THIS POWER OF ATTORNEY, YOU MUST COMPLETE THE CERTIFICATION OPPOSITE THE SIGNATURES OF THE AGENTS.)

Specimen signatures of agent          I certify that the signatures of my
(and successors)                      Agent (and successors) are correct.

_____        _____
(agent)                               (principal)

_____        _____
(successor agent)                     (principal)

_____        _____
(successor agent)                     (principal)

(B) The statutory short-form power of attorney for health care (the statutory health-care power) authorizes the agent to make any and all health-care decisions on behalf of the principal which the principal could make if present and under no disability, subject to any limitations on the granted powers that appear on the face of the form, to be exercised in such manner as the agent deems consistent with the intent and desires of the principal. The agent will be under no duty to exercise granted powers or to assume control of or responsibility for the principal's health care; but when granted powers are exercised, the agent will be required to use due care to act for the benefit of the principal in accordance with the terms of the statutory health-care power and will be liable for negligent exercise. The agent may act in person or through others reasonably employed by the agent for that purpose but may not delegate authority to make health-care decisions. The agent may sign and deliver all instruments, negotiate and enter into all agreements, and do all other acts reasonably necessary to implement the exercise of the powers granted to the agent. Without limiting the generality of the foregoing, the statutory health-care power shall include the following powers, subject to any limitations appearing on the face of the form:

(1) The agent is authorized to give consent to and authorize or refuse, or to withhold or withdraw consent to, any and all types of medical care, treatment or procedures relating to the physical or mental health of the principal, including any medication program, surgical procedures, life-sustaining treatment, or provision of food and fluids for the principal.

(2) The agent is authorized to admit the principal to or discharge the principal from any and all types of hospitals, institutions, homes, residential or nursing facilities, treatment centers, and health-care institutions providing personal care or treatment for any type of physical or mental condition. The agent shall have the same right to visit the principal in the hospital or other institution as is granted to a spouse or adult child of the principal, any rule of the institution to the contrary notwithstanding.

(3) The agent is authorized to contract for any and all types of health-care services and facilities in the name of and on behalf of the principal and to bind the principal to pay for all such services and facilities, and to have and exercise those powers over the principal's property as are authorized under the statutory property power, to the extent the agent deems necessary to pay health-care costs; and the agent shall not be personally liable for any services or care contracted for on behalf of the principal.

(4) At the principal's expense, and subject to reasonable rules of the health-care provider to prevent disruption of the principal's health care, the agent shall have the same right the principal has to examine and copy and consent to disclosure of all the principal's medical records that the agent deems relevant to the exercise of the agent's powers, whether the records relate to mental health or any other medical condition and whether they are in the possession of or maintained by any physician, psychiatrist, psychologist, therapist, hospital, nursing home, or other health-care provider.

(5) The agent is authorized: to direct that an autopsy be made pursuant to §2 of An Act in relation to autopsy of dead bodies, approved August 13, 1965 (410 ILCS 505/2), including all amendments; to make a disposition of any part or all of the principal's body pursuant to the Uniform Anatomical Gift Act (755 ILCS 50/1), as now or hereafter amended; and to direct the disposition of the principal's remains.

# Sample Living Will

This declaration is made this _____ day of _____, _____.

I, _____, being of sound mind, willfully and voluntarily make known my desire that my moment of death shall not be artificially postponed.

If at any time I should have an incurable and irreversible injury, disease, or illness judged to be a terminal condition by my attending physician who has personally examined me, and has determined that my death is imminent except for death-delaying procedures, I direct that such procedures which would only prolong the dying process be withheld or withdrawn, and that I be permitted to die naturally with only the administration of medication, sustenance, or the performance of any medical procedure deemed necessary by my attending physician to provide me with comfort care.

In the absence of my ability to give directions regarding the use of such death-delaying procedures, it is my intention that this declaration shall be honored by my family and physician as the final expression of my legal right to refuse medical or surgical treatment and accept the consequences from such refusal.

_____          _____
(Signature)                       (Date Signed)

STATE OF _____

CITY OF _____

COUNTY OF _____

The declarant is personally known to me and I believe h___ to be of sound mind. I saw the declarant sign the declaration in my presence and I signed the declaration as a witness in the presence of the declarant. I did not sign the declarant's signature above for or at the direction of the declarant. At the date of this instrument, I am not entitled to any portion of the estate of the declarant according to the laws of intestate succession or, to the best of my knowledge and belief, under any will of declarant or other instrument taking effect at declarant's death, or directly financially responsible for declarant's medical care.

Witness _____

Witness _____

# Personal Information
# Checklist

YOURSELF                                          SPOUSE

Full name          _____          _____
Date of birth      _____          _____
SSN                _____          _____
Principal          _____          _____
Residence          _____          _____

MARITAL STATUS
If married, date of marriage              _____
If spouse is deceased, date of death      _____
If divorced, date of divorce              _____

If divorced:
Full name of ex-spouse                    _____
Date of birth                             _____
SSN                                       _____
Address                                   _____
                                          _____

If deceased, date of death                _____
Children born of this marriage            _____
(names and ages)                          _____
                                          _____
                                          _____
                                          _____

CITIZENSHIP
Yourself _____ Spouse _____

## ESTATE-PLANNING OBJECTIVES

_____

_____

_____

_____

_____

_____

CHILDREN
Full name            _____
Date of birth (age)  _____
SSN                  _____
Address              _____
Phone                _____

Full name            _____
Date of birth (age)  _____
SSN                  _____
Address              _____
Phone                _____

Full name            _____
Date of birth (age)  _____
SSN                  _____
Address              _____
Phone                _____

Full name            _____
Date of birth (age)  _____

SSN _____

Address _____

Phone _____

GRANDCHILDREN

Full name _____

Date of birth (age) _____

SSN _____

Address _____

Phone _____

Full name _____

Date of birth (age) _____

SSN _____

Address _____

Phone _____

DEPENDENT (list any individuals dependent on you for support)

Full name _____

Date of birth (age) _____

SSN _____

Address _____

Trust name _____

ADVISORS

**Accountant** (tax-return preparer)

Name _____

Firm _____

Phone _____

**Attorney**

Name _____

Firm _____

Phone _____

**Insurance Agent**

Name _____

Firm _____

Phone _____

## Certified Financial Planner
Name                _____

Firm                  _____

Phone              _____

## Investment Advisor
Name                _____

Firm                  _____

Phone              _____

## Banker
Name                _____

Firm                  _____

Phone              _____

## Doctor or HMO
Name                _____

Firm                  _____

Phone              _____

## Clergy
Name                _____

Church           _____

Phone              _____

ESTATE OFFICEHOLDERS

## Executor
Name                _____

Phone              _____

Address          _____

## Successor Executor
Name                _____

Phone              _____

Address           _____

## Guardian
Name                _____

Phone              _____

Address           _____

## Successor Guardian
Name     _____

Phone     _____

Address     _____

## Trustee of Minor Children's Assets
Name     _____

Phone     _____

Address     _____

## Successor Trustee of Minor Children's Assets
Name     _____

Phone     _____

Address     _____

## Agent on Durable Power of Attorney for Property
Name     _____

Address     _____

Phone     _____

Restrictions     _____

## Agent on Health-Care Power of Attorney for Property
Name     _____

Address     _____

Phone     _____

Restrictions     _____

## BENEFICIARIES
Full name     _____

Phone     _____

Address     _____

Bequest     _____

Full name     _____

Phone     _____

Address     _____

Bequest     _____

Full name          _____

Phone              _____

Address            _____

Bequest            _____


Full name          _____

Phone              _____

Address            _____

Bequest            _____


Full name          _____

Phone              _____

Address            _____

Bequest            _____


CHARITIES (Names of charitable foundations you would like to support)

Name               _____

Phone              _____

Address            _____

Amount             _____


PREPAID FUNERAL ARRANGEMENTS

Funeral home       _____

Person to contact  _____

Address            _____

Phone              _____

Location of
cemetery plot      _____


PROPERTY

**Personal Residence**

Address            _____

Type of deed       _____

Co-owners          _____

Current value      _____

Purchase price     _____

Insurance policy   _____

Mortgage holder    _____

Amount _____

PIN number _____

Insurance _____

**Vacation Home**

Address _____

Type of deed _____

Co-owners _____

Current value _____

Purchase price _____

Insurance policy _____

Mortgage holder _____

Amount _____

PIN number _____

Insurance _____

**Other real estate**

Address _____

Type of deed _____

Co-owners _____

Current value _____

Purchase price _____

Insurance policy _____

Mortgage holder _____

Amount _____

PIN number _____

Insurance _____

**Vehicles**

Co-owner _____

Lien holder _____

Insurance policy _____

**Safe-Deposit Boxes**

Location of keys _____

Names on boxes _____

Bank names
and addresses _____

INSURANCE POLICIES

**Homeowners**

Issuer/policy #     _____

Agent/number     _____

**Vehicles**

Issuer/policy #     _____

Agent/number     _____

**Health**

Issuer/policy #     _____

Agent/number     _____

**Life insurance**

Issuer/policy #     _____

Agent/number     _____

FINANCES

**Individual Retirement Accounts**

Trustee name     _____

Beneficiary     _____

Account number     _____

**Deferred Compensation Accounts**

Trustee name     _____

Beneficiary     _____

Account number     _____

**Certificates of Deposit**

Bank or holder     _____

CD number     _____

Bank or holder     _____

CD number     _____

**Checking/Savings/Money Market Accounts**

Type/amount     _____

Location     _____

Account number     _____

Type/amount _____

Location _____

Account number _____

Type/amount _____

Location _____

Account number _____

## Savings Bonds

Type/amount _____

Location _____

Interest paid to date _____

## Stocks/Bonds/Annuities

Type/amount _____

Location _____

Account number _____

Type/amount _____

Location _____

Account number _____

Type/amount _____

Location _____

Account number _____

## Closely Held Business Interest

Description _____

Buy/sell agreement? _____

Stock redemption
Agreement? _____

Valuation _____

Family members
involved in business _____

## Beneficial Interest in a Trust (to include any power of appointment)

Name of trust _____

Description _____

Type/date _____

Location of
agreement        _____
Trustee          _____

**Expectancies** (if you are named in a will)
Name of person   _____
Relationship     _____

**Other Personal Property** (with value in excess of $5,000)
Description       _____
Description       _____
Description       _____
Description       _____
Description       _____

**Out-of-State Property**
Address           _____
Deed              _____
Co-owners         _____
Purchase price    _____
Market value      _____

**Partnership Property**
Address           _____
Description of
interest and cost _____
Successor in
interest          _____

DEBTS
**Charge Cards**
Company           _____
Account number    _____
Phone to cancel   _____

Company           _____
Account number    _____
Phone to cancel   _____

Company _____

Account number _____

Phone to cancel _____

## Loans

Company _____

Account number _____

Phone to cancel _____

Company _____

Account number _____

Phone to cancel _____

Company _____

Account number _____

Phone to cancel _____

Company _____

Account number _____

Phone to cancel _____

Company _____

Account number _____

Phone to cancel _____

## PROPERTY PLEDGED OR GUARANTEED

Description _____

Amount _____

Company _____

## OTHER DEBTS

Description _____

Amount _____

Company _____

## POTENTIAL TAX DEFICIENCIES (for example, if your returns are under audit)

Tax years under audit _____

## LITIGATION AND JUDGMENTS

Description _____

Amount _____

Law Firm _____

# Administration Checklist

ESTATE OF _____ _____

Date of death _____ Place of death _____
Cause of death _____

Executor
Name _____ _____
Address _____
Phone/Fax _____ _____

|  | Decedent | Spouse |
|--|----------|--------|

Decedent          Spouse

Name _____ _____
SSN _____ _____
Permanent address
_____ _____
_____ _____
_____ _____

Date of birth
_____ _____

Place of birth
_____ _____

Citizenship

_____          _____

If retired, give date

_____          _____

Last date of work

_____          _____


CHILDREN
Name    _____          _____
SSN     _____          _____
Age and date of birth

_____          _____


Name    _____          _____
SSN     _____          _____
Age and date of birth

_____          _____


Name    _____          _____
SSN     _____          _____
Age and date of birth

_____          _____


Name    _____          _____
SSN     _____          _____
Age and date of birth

_____          _____


Name    _____          _____
SSN     _____          _____
Age and date of birth

_____          _____


DOCTORS AND HOSPITALS
Hospital: name and address _____
Doctor: name and address  _____
Doctor: name and address  _____
All paid with receipts?   _____

## INCOME-TAX DATA (Form 1040)

Income tax returns filed for prior years? _____

Prior year's returns under audit? _____

Date current income tax return due: _____

Tax information authorization, Form 8821, filed with IRS? _____

Amount of estimated tax payments made this year: _____

## GIFT-TAX RETURNS (Form 709)

Did decedent file any gift tax returns in prior years? _____

## TRUST RETURNS (Form 1041)

Trusts in which decedent had an interest

| Trust Name | Tax ID number | Due Date | Date Filed |
|---|---|---|---|
| _____ | _____ | _____ | _____ |
| _____ | _____ | _____ | _____ |
| _____ | _____ | _____ | _____ |
| _____ | _____ | _____ | _____ |
| _____ | _____ | _____ | _____ |

## ESTATE- AND GIFT-TAX RETURNS

Form 706 due date _____

State inheritance tax-return due date _____

Extensions requested to pay tax? _____

## ADMINISTRATION

Date will filed with clerk's office _____

Contract signed with attorney to handle probate? _____

Is the contract based on an hourly basis or percentage? _____

| Attorney Name | Address | Phone | Fax |
|---|---|---|---|
| _____ | _____ | _____ | _____ |

Ancillary (out of state) probate required? _____

| Attorney Name | Address | Phone | Fax |
|---|---|---|---|
| _____ | _____ | _____ | _____ |

Date safe-deposit boxes inventoried _____

Parties present _____

Spouse award; amount and date paid     _____

Minor child awards; amounts and dates paid     _____

_____

_____

_____

## PROBATE PROCEEDINGS

Court docket number     _____

Date Letters of Office Issued     _____

Claim cutoff date     _____

Date notice placed in paper     _____

Inventory filed with court     _____

| | Name of Creditor | Date Notified | Date Paid | Amount Paid |
|---|---|---|---|---|
| Creditors (and claims filed) | \_\_\_\_\_ | \_\_\_\_\_ | \_\_\_\_\_ | \_\_\_\_\_ |
| List reason contested | \_\_\_\_\_ | \_\_\_\_\_ | \_\_\_\_\_ | \_\_\_\_\_ |
| if not paid | \_\_\_\_\_ | \_\_\_\_\_ | \_\_\_\_\_ | \_\_\_\_\_ |
| | \_\_\_\_\_ | \_\_\_\_\_ | \_\_\_\_\_ | \_\_\_\_\_ |
| | \_\_\_\_\_ | \_\_\_\_\_ | \_\_\_\_\_ | \_\_\_\_\_ |
| | \_\_\_\_\_ | \_\_\_\_\_ | \_\_\_\_\_ | \_\_\_\_\_ |
| | \_\_\_\_\_ | \_\_\_\_\_ | \_\_\_\_\_ | \_\_\_\_\_ |
| | \_\_\_\_\_ | \_\_\_\_\_ | \_\_\_\_\_ | \_\_\_\_\_ |

| Specific Legacies | Name of Person Paid | Date Paid | Amount Receipt? |
|---|---|---|---|
| \_\_\_\_\_ | \_\_\_\_\_ | \_\_\_\_\_ | \_\_\_\_\_ |
| \_\_\_\_\_ | \_\_\_\_\_ | \_\_\_\_\_ | \_\_\_\_\_ |
| \_\_\_\_\_ | \_\_\_\_\_ | \_\_\_\_\_ | \_\_\_\_\_ |
| \_\_\_\_\_ | \_\_\_\_\_ | \_\_\_\_\_ | \_\_\_\_\_ |
| \_\_\_\_\_ | \_\_\_\_\_ | \_\_\_\_\_ | \_\_\_\_\_ |
| \_\_\_\_\_ | \_\_\_\_\_ | \_\_\_\_\_ | \_\_\_\_\_ |
| \_\_\_\_\_ | \_\_\_\_\_ | \_\_\_\_\_ | \_\_\_\_\_ |

| Beneficiaries | Name of Person Paid | Date Paid | Amount Receipt? |
|---|---|---|---|
| _____ | _____ | _____ | _____ |
| _____ | _____ | _____ | _____ |
| _____ | _____ | _____ | _____ |
| _____ | _____ | _____ | _____ |
| _____ | _____ | _____ | _____ |
| _____ | _____ | _____ | _____ |

## PROPERTY

\* Enter name and address of appraiser if necessary.

\*\* List if asset is owned individually, jointly, tenants in common, community property, or held in trust

| Description | Location/Contact | Value* | Ownership** | Date |
|---|---|---|---|---|
| _____ | _____ | _____ | _____ | _____ |
| _____ | _____ | _____ | _____ | _____ |
| _____ | _____ | _____ | _____ | _____ |
| _____ | _____ | _____ | _____ | _____ |
| _____ | _____ | _____ | _____ | _____ |
| _____ | _____ | _____ | _____ | _____ |
| _____ | _____ | _____ | _____ | _____ |
| _____ | _____ | _____ | _____ | _____ |
| _____ | _____ | _____ | _____ | _____ |
| _____ | _____ | _____ | _____ | _____ |
| _____ | _____ | _____ | _____ | _____ |

## DEBTS

| Description | Account | Amount | Date Paid |
|---|---|---|---|
| _____ | _____ | _____ | _____ |
| _____ | _____ | _____ | _____ |
| _____ | _____ | _____ | _____ |
| _____ | _____ | _____ | _____ |
| _____ | _____ | _____ | _____ |
| _____ | _____ | _____ | _____ |
| _____ | _____ | _____ | _____ |

# Sample Small Estate Affidavit

State of _____ ) ss
County of _____ )

I, _____, being duly sworn, hereby state:

1. My post office address and telephone number are:

_____        (___)_____

_____

_____

I understand that if no person is named above as my agent for service, or, if for any reason service on the named person cannot be effectuated, the Clerk of the Circuit Court of _____ County _____ is recognized by _____ law as my agent for service of process.

2. The decedent's name is _____ .

3. The date of the decedent's death was _____,
and I have attached a copy of the death certificate hereto;

4. The decedent's place of residence immediately before h__ death was:

_____

_____

_____

5. No letters of office are now outstanding on the decedent's estate and no petition for letters is contemplated or pending in _____ or in any other jurisdiction, to my knowledge.

6. The gross value of the decedent's entire personal estate, including the value of all property passing to any party either by intestacy or under a will, does not exceed $_____. The personal property not subject to probate and passing under h__ will is as follows:

| Item | Approximate value |
|------|-------------------|
| _____ | $_____ |
| _____ | _____ |
| _____ | _____ |
| _____ | _____ |
| Total | $_____ |

7. All of the decedent's funeral expenses (have) (have not) been paid.

8. There is no known unpaid claimant or contested claim against the estate.

9. The names and places of residence of any surviving spouse, minor children, and adult dependent children of the decedent are as follows:

| Name | Age | Relationship |
|------|-----|--------------|
| _____ | ____ | _____ |
| _____ | ____ | _____ |
| _____ | ____ | _____ |
| _____ | ____ | _____ |

10. The decedent left a will, which has been filed with the Clerk of the Circuit Court of _____ County. A certified copy of the will on file is attached. To the best of my knowledge and belief, the will on file is the decedent's last will and was signed by the decedent and the attesting witnesses as required by law, and would be admittable to probate. The names and places of residence of the legatees and the portion of the estate, if any, to which each legatee is entitled are as follows:

| Name | Age | Percentage |
|------|-----|------------|
| _____ | ____ | _____ |
| _____ | ____ | _____ |
| _____ | ____ | _____ |
| _____ | ____ | _____ |

The affiant is (aware) (unaware) of any dispute or potential conflict as to the heirship or will of the decedent.

11. The property described in paragraph 6 of this affidavit should be distributed as follows:

| Name | Age | Percentage |
|------|-----|------------|
| _____ | ____ | _____ |
| _____ | ____ | _____ |
| _____ | ____ | _____ |
| _____ | ____ | _____ |

The foregoing statement is made under the penalties of perjury.


BY: _____
(Name)


State of _____) ss
County of _____)

SUBSCRIBED AND SWORN TO before me this _____ day of

_____, _____.



_____

NOTARY PUBLIC


I, _____, Attorney at Law, duly licensed to practice law in the State of _____ have prepared the foregoing affidavit on behalf of the party signing it. Further, based on the information supplied to me, which I have no reason to believe is not true and accurate, paragraphs 9 through 11 correctly reflect the appropriate heirship and distributions under the applicable law and any will.

_____

_____

_____

(Name and address of attorney)

# K

# Sample Last Will and Testament

LAST WILL AND TESTAMENT

OF

_____

I, _____, of the City of _____, County of _____, and State of _____, being of sound mind and memory, publish and declare this to be my Last Will and Testament, and I hereby revoke all prior Wills and Codicils made by me.

FIRST

I am married to _____, and all references in this Will to my spouse are to h_____. At the present time, I have _____ children, however, all references in this Will to my children shall include any child born or adopted by me after the date of execution of this Will. My children's names and ages as of the date of this Will are as follows:

_____

_____

_____

SECOND

I hereby order and direct my executor, named in paragraph SIXTH:

(A)      To pay all my just debts and funeral expenses as soon after my death as practicable;

(B)      To pay all federal, state, and local, income and estate taxes, which my executor may be required to pay out of my estate, and which shall be treated as an expense and cost of administering my estate and shall be paid before the distribution of my estate. My executor shall have no rights, duty, or obligation to obtain reimbursement for any taxes paid or expenses incurred in connection therewith, even though not on property passing under this Will;

(C)      To reimburse any of my beneficiaries who have advanced, out of their own funds, any money or paid any bills for my last illness or death on my behalf, if possible, before the distribution of my estate; if it is not possible to reimburse them before the distribution of my estate, then the amounts they have so advanced or paid shall be deducted from any specific gifts made in this Will and my beneficiaries' shares in equal proportions;

_____

(Initials and date)

(D)      Where possible and in the sole judgment of my executor, I direct my executor to satisfy any charitable bequests I have made with Income in Respect of a Decedent property and satisfy individual bequests with non-Income in Respect of a Decedent property, provided such individual bequests are not decreased, and provided the purpose of any charitable trust is not affected;

(E)      The full power and authority to settle any and all claims for or against my estate, and to execute and deliver all proper and necessary conveyances to sell and dispose any and all assets of my estate, including real estate without order of any court;

(F)      The full power and authority provided for under Internal Revenue Code §2631 or any successor section thereto regarding the Generation Skipping Transfer (GST) exemption, to determine the inclusion ratio which my executor deems fair and equitable in h_____ judgment with respect to any property for which I have not previously determined a GST inclusion ratio; and

(G)    The full power and authority necessary to operate, manage, and perform all acts to continue any business interest I may have until such interests can be distributed in a timely manner to my beneficiaries.

THIRD

I hereby provide for the sum of _____ to be paid to my executor as reasonable compensation for h_____ services. Such compensation shall be paid after the expenses of my estate but prior to distribution of any specific gifts or distributions to beneficiaries.

FOURTH

After the payment of my debts as described above, I hereby give, devise and bequeath the following specific gifts:

_____

_____

_____

_____

_____

If a beneficiary named in this paragraph shall predecease me, then that specific gift described in this paragraph shall fail.

_____

(Initials and date)

FIFTH

After the payment of my debts, compensation to the executor, and specific gifts as described above, I hereby give, devise, and bequeath all the rest of my estate, of whatever kind and wherever situated, both real and personal, and any over which I may have the power of testamentary disposition, to my spouse. In the event that my spouse predeceases me, or dies within thirty (30) days of my death, I hereby give, devise, and bequeath all the rest of my estate, of whatever kind and wherever situated, in equal shares per stirpes, as follows:

_____

_____

_____

SIXTH

I hereby name my spouse to act as executor. In the event my spouse is unable or unwilling to act as executor, I name _____ _____, to act as successor executor. I hereby waive the surety on my executor's bond.

SEVENTH

In the event that my spouse predeceases me, or dies after my death without making provision for the care and custody of our minor children, if any, I nominate and appoint _____, to act as guardian of all of my minor children. In the event he or she is unable or unwilling to act as guardian, I nominate and appoint _____, to act as guardian. I hereby waive the surety on the guardian's bond.

EIGHTH

If any beneficiary of mine is less than twenty-one (21) years of age, their specific gifts as described in paragraph FOURTH, if any, and their share of my estate shall immediately vest, but the distribution thereof shall be held in trust by the trustee named in paragraph NINTH, and the distribution thereof shall be deferred as follows: ⅓ of the principal of the trust shall be distributed to each such beneficiary at the age of twenty-one (21) years, ⅓ of the principal of the trust shall be distributed at the age of twenty-five (25) years, and the remaining principal and income, if any, shall be distributed at the age of twenty-eight (28) years. If, after any such beneficiary shall reach the age of twenty-one (21) years, the balance of a trust for their benefit shall be less than twenty-five thousand dollars ($25,000), their trust shall be terminated and the principal and income distributed to them as soon as possible. In the meantime, the trustee shall pay on

_____

(Initials and date)

a quarterly basis the net income earned by each beneficiaries' trust to each such beneficiary.

NINTH

I hereby name _____, to act as trustee of any and all minor's trusts as described in paragraph EIGHTH. In the event

he or she is unable or unwilling to act as trustee, I name
_____, to act as successor trustee. I hereby
waive the surety on my trustee's bond.

TENTH

In the event my spouse and beneficiaries shall predecease me leaving no
descendants, I hereby give, devise, and bequeath all the rest of my property, of whatever kind and wherever situated, in equal shares per stirpes, as
follows:

(Initials and date)

IN WITNESS WHEREOF, I have signed this, my Last Will and Testament,
consisting of ____ typewritten pages, counting this page but not counting
the Notary Public Certification page following, on this _____ day of
_____, _____.

Testator(ix)

We, the undersigned, hereby certify that on the date above written, the Testator(ix) signed this instrument in our presence and declared this to be h____ Last Will and Testament, and we, at the Testator(ix)'s request and in the Testator(ix)'s presence and the presence of each other hereby sign as witnesses, declaring the Testator(ix) to be of sound mind and under no duress and above the age of eighteen (18) years of age.

NAME                         ADDRESS

_____     _____

                                 _____

                                 _____

_____     _____

                                 _____

                                 _____

                                 _____

                                 (Initials and date)

State of _____) ss.
County of _____)

The undersigned, a notary public in and for the above county and state, certifies that _____, the above subscribed Testator(ix), and _____ and _____, the above subscribed witnesses, all said persons having been first duly sworn by me, the Testator(ix) _____ declared in my presence and the presence of the witnesses this instrument was h____ Last Will and Testament and that this instrument is being executed as a free and voluntary act. The foregoing witnesses stated they have been asked by the Testator(ix) to subscribe as witnesses, that they heard the Testator(ix) declare this instrument to be h____ Last Will and Testament, and they saw the Testator(ix) sign this instrument in their presence, and upon their oaths state they did sign as witnesses, and on the date signed by the Testator(ix) the witnesses declare the Testator(ix) to be of sound mind and under no constraint and above the age of eighteen (18) years of age. The witnesses also each declared they are on this date above the age of eighteen (18) years of age.

Dated:                          _____

(Seal)                          _____

Notary Public

My commission expires     _____

This document was prepared by:

# Sample Living Trust Agreement

LIVING TRUST AGREEMENT
OF

_____

I, _____, of the State of _____, hereafter called Grantor, transfer property listed in the attached Exhibit A to myself as trustee, and as trustee agree to hold, manage, and distribute said property and any other property added thereto in trust (hereinafter called a Trust Estate) upon the terms and conditions of this agreement.

FIRST:

1. During Grantor's lifetime, the trustee shall pay to Grantor the entire net income of the Trust Estate. Grantor shall have the right at all times:

(a) To modify and amend this Agreement;

(b) To terminate this or any trust created by this Agreement in whole or in part; and

(c) To add other property to the Trust Estate.

Every modification or amendment to this agreement shall be effective when signed by Grantor but no change in the duties, powers, or liabilities of any trustee shall become effective until such trustee consents to such change.

2. If at any time the trustee shall determine that Grantor is unable to exercise h___ rights under this agreement, or lack capacity as provided for

in paragraph NINTH, the trustee may pay to Grantor or, even if a guardian has been appointed, apply for Grantor's care, comfort, support, maintenance, medical, and hospital care as the trustee deems best.

3.   After Grantor's death, the trustee may accept additional property from any source, including property from Grantor's will, and shall hold, manage, and distribute such property, together with all other property held in trust as provided for in this agreement.

SECOND:
Grantor hereby directs the trustee to pay the expenses of Grantor's last illness and funeral and any income, estate, or inheritance taxes, becoming due because of Grantor's death including deficiencies, interest, and penalties. The foregoing direction respecting payment of federal estate taxes shall apply only to the extent that the payments exceed the face value of any bond owned by Grantor at death, redeemable at par to pay such taxes. Grantor hereby directs the trustee not to seek reimbursement, contribution, or apportionment for any payment so made even with respect to property passing outside this trust. If the assets of Grantor's estate subject to probate (excluding tangible personal property and any assets specifically bequeathed or devised by will or any codicil thereto) are insufficient to pay any legacies set forth in Grantor's will or codicil, the trustee shall pay such legacies. The provisions of this article shall not vest in any creditor or third party any interest in or right to any part of the principal of the Trust Estate.

THIRD:
1.   After Grantor's death, the trustee shall pay the Trust Estate and all accrued net income as follows:

_____

_____

_____

_____

_____

_____

_____

_____

_____

If a beneficiary listed above should predecease Grantor or die before complete distribution thereof, their interest shall be paid to their descendants per stirpes and if there be none, to be added to the remaining beneficiaries in the same ratio each remaining bears to the whole.

2.   If the trustee shall be holding the Trust Estate, or any portion thereof, which shall not have vested or otherwise become distributable under any other provision of Grantor's trust at a time when no beneficiary of Grantor shall be living, the trustee shall pay and distribute the same to Grantor's then-living heirs at law, determined in accordance with the then existing statutes of the State of _____ governing the intestate distribution of property.

FOURTH:

If, under the preceding paragraph, any portion of the principal of a trust becomes payable to any beneficiary who is less than twenty-one (21) years of age and for whose benefit the trustee is not then holding a separate trust, such portion shall immediately vest in such beneficiary, but the distribution thereof shall be postponed until such beneficiary attains the age of twenty-one (21) years, and, in the meantime, the trustee shall hold the same as a separate trust and pay the net income therefrom to such beneficiary.

FIFTH:

1.   Whenever any beneficiary of the Trust Estate, or of any separate trust derived therefrom, to whom payments of income or principal are herein authorized or directed to be made, is under a legal disability or in the sole judgment of the trustee, is otherwise unable to apply such payments for the beneficiary's own best interest and advantage, the trustee may
(a)  Make any portion of such payments as follows:
    (i)   Directly to such beneficiary;
    (ii)  To the legal guardian or conservator of such beneficiary;
    (iii) To a relative of such beneficiary to be expended by such relative for the benefit of such beneficiary;
    (iv)  To a custodian to be held for the benefit of such beneficiary pursuant to a Uniform Gifts to Minors Act or comparable statute of any state; or
    (v)   By expending the same for the benefit of such beneficiary;

(b)  Withhold all or any portion of any income payments not necessary for the suitable care, comfort, support, maintenance, and medical care of such beneficiary. The decision in each case shall be made solely by the trustee.

2.    If at any time in the judgment of the trustee, the aggregate of the income payable hereunder to any beneficiary to whom income may then be paid hereunder, and all other resources known to the trustee to be readily available to such beneficiary shall be insufficient to provide for h____ suitable care, comfort, support, maintenance, education, and medical care; the trustee in its discretion may pay to or apply for the use and benefit of such beneficiary for such purpose any part or all of the principal of such trust.

SIXTH:
With respect to each trust under this instrument:

(1)  The interest of any beneficiary hereunder shall not be subject to attachment for whatever cause, nor to the claims of creditors, and, except for the exercise of any Powers of Appointment granted, may not be transferred, assigned, or encumbered.

(2)  Unless otherwise provided, the word "trustee" as used herein shall include any successor trustee. No bond, surety, or security shall be required of any trustee. The plural term "descendants" shall include the singular; words imparting a particular number or gender shall include other numbers and gender; any person born out of lawful wedlock remaining illegitimate at the date of Grantor's death, together with the descendants of such person's ancestors; and a lawfully adopted person shall be treated as a natural legitimate child of such person's adopting parent.

(3)  A Power of Appointment granted by this agreement shall include the power to create additional powers and to appoint outright or in trust. The trustee may rely upon the order of any court admitting an instrument to probate as the will of a holder of a Power of Appointment granted herein, or the finding of any court that such holder died intestate, or may assume such power was not exercised in the absence of actual notice of such holder's will or probate proceedings within three months after such holder's death; provided, however, that this paragraph shall not affect any right

which an appointee or beneficiary in default of appointment may have against anyone to whom the trustee may have made distribution.

(4) The trustee in its discretion may terminate at any time any trust which has an aggregate principal value of twenty-five thousand dollars ($25,000) or less.

(5) Any trust still in existence on the day preceding the day twenty-one (21) years after the death of the last to survive of all the beneficiaries herein named or described who are living at the date of Grantor's death shall forthwith terminate.

SEVENTH:
The trustee shall have the full power and authority as provided for under the statutes of the State of _____, to include but not limited to the following:

(1) To allot to any trust created hereunder an undivided interest in any property constituting a portion of a trust; to make joint investments; to make any division or distribution in kind partly in kind and partly in money and to determine the value of any property so allotted, divided or distributed;

(2) To sell, exchange, lease for any period not exceeding ninety-nine (99) years, mortgage or pledge any property, real or personal, at any time constituting a portion of a trust; to create liens of any type on any trust; upon such terms as the trustee shall deem wise;

(3) To write or purchase put and covered call option contracts;

(4) To invest any money in a trust in such property, real or personal, as the trustee shall deem wise, without being limited by any rule of law regarding investment by trustees;

(5) To retain, without incurring any liability, as investments of a trust any property owned by Grantor at the time of Grantor's death as long as the trustee shall deem wise;

(6) To cause any property which may at any time constitute a portion of a trust to be issued, held or registered, certificated or not, in the name of

the trustee, in the name of a nominee or in such other form; to place any such property in the custody of a depository or clearing corporation;

(7) To exercise or not exercise all the rights and powers of an individual owner with respect to shares of stock, bonds, or other securities in the trust;

(8) To borrow money for any purpose and to mortgage or pledge any trust property;

(9) To employ attorneys and agents and delegate to them necessary powers;

(10) To pay all costs, taxes, expenses, and fees in connection with the administration of a trust, including a reasonable compensation to the trustee and attorneys and agents;

(11) To determine what is "income" and what is "principal" hereunder, except:
  (a)  any interest or dividend received on any securities held, which is accrued and unpaid at the time of the delivery of such security to the trustee shall be considered as income;
  (b)  in the case of securities purchased at a discount, the entire subsequent sale price or maturity value shall be credited to principal;
  (c)  in the case of securities purchased at a premium, the trustee shall charge the premium against principal without amortizing the same;
  (d)  any stock dividend or subscription right which may be declared upon or issued in connection with any stock constituting a portion of a trust shall be considered as principal;
  (e)  in the case of real estate, the trustee shall not create a reserve for depreciation;

(12) To postpone distribution from a trust pending final disposition of all liabilities relating to such trust and to convert any or all assets thereof to cash pending such disposition;

(13) To vote or refrain from voting, in person or by and through a proxy, any security or other asset having voting rights without limitation; if,

however, the trustee's possession of voting rights with respect to any holding or the retention of such security would adversely affect the entity represented by such holding or any trustee's ability to retain or vote such holding by reason of any law, rule, or regulation, then the trustee shall vote such holding upon and only in accordance with the written directions of a majority in interest of the beneficiaries then entitled to receive the income from the trust holding such asset;

(14) To purchase securities and other property from Grantor's estate and from Grantor's family and to make loans to such legal representative if the trustee in its sole judgment determines that such purchase or loan is advisable, and the trustee shall not be liable for any loss resulting thereto;

(15) To merge any trust with any other trust having terms and beneficiaries which are substantially identical and to hold them as a single trust insofar as practical;

(16) To determine the inclusion ratio which the trustee deems fair and equitable in h____ judgment with respect to any property for which Grantor has not previously determined a Generation Skipping Transfer (GST) tax inclusion ratio as provided for under Internal Revenue Code §2631 or any successor section thereto;

(17) To continue the business interests of Grantor with the full power and authority necessary to operate, manage, and perform all necessary acts until such interests can be distributed in a timely manner to Grantor's beneficiaries; and

(18) To do all other acts which in the judgment of the trustee are necessary or desirable for the proper and advantageous management, investment, and distribution of each trust.

EIGHTH:
With respect to the trustee of each trust created under this agreement:

(1)  Any trustee may resign by delivering a written resignation to a majority in interest of the beneficiaries to whom income from such separate trust may then be paid hereunder. A majority in interest of the beneficiaries then entitled to receive income from any separate trust hereunder, or

the individual trustee of such separate trust, if any, may, without liability to any present or future beneficiary of any trust created hereunder, approve the accounts of and give a full complete release and discharge to any such trustee and to the legal representative of any deceased or legally disabled individual trustee. Such persons have the right without the concurrence of any remainderman or other party in interest to determine on behalf of all beneficiaries, the propriety of giving any such approval, release and discharge, notwithstanding that their interest may possibly be or become adverse to those of other beneficiaries. Such approval, release, and discharge shall have the same effect as a final decree of a court of competent jurisdiction. The legal representative of the estate, the parent or guardian of any beneficiary under the disability shall receive notice for and may act on behalf of such beneficiary under this paragraph.

(2)   All trustees acting from time to time shall have the same powers, duties, and discretions herein conferred or imposed upon the trustee named. No successor trustee shall be liable or responsible for any acts or defaults of any predecessor trustee or for any losses or expenses resulting from any action or omission in the prior administration of any trust.

(3)   The trustee shall not be liable: (a) for any loss, claim, expense, liability, or damage to any trust or property held in trust to any beneficiary caused by the trustee in the good-faith omission or exercise of any of its powers, duties, and discretions, including but not limited to reliance upon the opinion of any attorney or accountant; or (b) for the acts or omissions of any agent, attorney or accountant; provided always that any person employed by the trustee must be selected with due care. Prior to delivering assets to a successor trustee or to making any partial or complete distribution of principal hereunder (other than a distribution which is made in the exercise of the trustee's discretion and does not terminate the trust), the trustee may require an approval of the trustee's accounts and a release and discharge from all beneficiaries having an interest in the distribution, or may require court settlement of such accounts. All of the trustee's fees and expenses, including attorney's fees, attributable to court approval of such accounts shall be paid by the trust.

(4)   Upon Grantor's death, resignation or other inability to act, the following shall thereafter act as trustee(s) hereunder in the order named:

(a) _____

(b) _____

(c) _____

(5)  A trustee may be removed from acting as trustee from any and all trusts by a vote of the majority in interest of the beneficiaries to whom income from such separate trust may then be paid. The beneficiaries shall approve the accounts of and give a full complete release and discharge to any removed trustee or to the legal representative of any deceased or legally disabled individual trustee. Such majority in interest of the beneficiaries shall have the right to remove a trustee without the concurrence of any remainderman or other party in interest. The legal representative of the estate, the parent or guardian of any beneficiary under a disability, shall receive notice for and may act on behalf of such beneficiary under this paragraph. The removal of a trustee or trustees shall not imply or indicate any negligence, malfeasance, or mismanagement. This section applies to both individuals and corporations acting as trustees. Removal of a trustee shall be in writing, signed by all beneficiaries who agree, and be sent by certified or registered mail, delivered to the trustee at their principal place of business or residence and shall become effective five (5) business days after receipt.

NINTH:

Grantor shall be considered unable to act if under a legal disability or, through illness, age, or other cause, is unable to give a reasoned consideration to financial matters. The existence of such inability may be determined by the principal physician attending to Grantor's care, and any person may rely upon written notice of such determination.

IN WITNESS WHEREOF, I have signed this Declaration of Trust this _____ day of _____, _____.


_____

Grantor

I hereby accept the foregoing terms, trusts, and conditions as of the date hereinabove written.

_____

Trustee

We hereby certify that the foregoing Declaration of Trust was signed by the Grantor and trustee in our joint presence, and at the request of and in the presence of the Grantor, trustee, and each other we subscribed our names as witnesses of the execution thereof on the date above written, and we certify that at the time of the execution hereof we are above the age of eighteen (18) years of age and we believe the Grantor and trustee to be of sound mind and under no constraints.

SIGNATURE                     RESIDENCE

_____       _____

                                    _____

_____       _____

                                    _____

_____       _____

                                    _____

SUBSCRIBED AND SWORN TO before me this _____ day of _____, _____.

_____

Notary Public

My commission expires: _____

This document was prepared by:

# Index

# Books from Allworth Press

**Your Living Trust and Estate Plan: How to Maximize Your Family's Assets and Protect Your Loved Ones** by Harvey J. Platt (softcover, 6 × 9, 304 pages, $14.95)

**The Retirement Handbook: How to Maximize Your Assets and Protect Your Quality of Life** by Carl Battle (softcover, 6 × 9, 240 pages, $18.95)

**Winning the Divorce War: How to Protect Your Best Interests** by Ronald Sharp (softcover, 6 × 9, 192 pages, $14.95)

**The Advertising Law Guide: A Friendly Guide for Everyone in Advertising** by Lee Wilson (softcover, 6 × 9, 272 pages, $19.95)

**The Copyright Guide: A Friendly Guide to Protecting and Profiting from Copyrights, Revised Edition** by Lee Wilson (softcover, 6 × 9, 208 pages, $18.95)

**The Trademark Guide: A Friendly Guide to Protecting and Profiting from Trademarks** by Lee Wilson (softcover, 6 × 9, 192 pages, $19.95)

**The Patent Guide: A Friendly Guide to Protecting and Profiting from Patents** by Carl W. Battle (softcover, 6 × 9, 224 pages, $18.95)

**The Soul of the New Consumer: The Attitudes, Behaviors, and Preferences of E-Customers** by Laurie Windham with Ken Orton (hardcover, 6¼ × 9¼, 320 pages, $24.95)

**Emotional Branding: The New Paradigm for Connecting Brands to People** by Marc Gobé (hardcover, 6¼ × 9¼, 352 pages, $24.95)

**The Entrepreneurial Age: Awakening the Spirit of Enterprise in People, Companies, and Countries** by Larry C. Farrell (hardcover, 6¼ × 9¼, 352 pages, $24.95)

**Money Secrets of the Rich and Famous** by Michael Reynard (hardcover, 6¼ × 9¼, 256 pages, $24.95)

**Dead Ahead: The Web Dilemma and the New Rules of Business** by Laurie Windham with John Samsel (softcover, 6¼ × 9¼, 256 pages, $24.95)

Please write to request our free catalog. To order by credit card, call 1-800-491-2808 or send a check or money order to Allworth Press, 10 East 23rd Street, Suite 510, New York, NY 10010. Include $5 for shipping and handling for the first book ordered and $1 for each additional book. Ten dollars plus $1 for each additional book if ordering from Canada. New York State residents must add sales tax.

To see our complete catalog on the World Wide Web, or to order online, you can find us at *www.allworth.com*.